URBAN ORIGINS OF AMERICAN JUDAISM

GEORGE H. SHRIVER

LECTURE SERIES IN

RELIGION IN

AMERICAN HISTORY

NO. 6

URBAN ORIGINS OF AMERICAN JUDAISM

Deborah Dash Moore

THE UNIVERSITY OF
GEORGIA PRESS
Athens and London

Athens, Georgia 30602
www.ugapress.org

Set in 10/14 Quadraat by Graphic Composition, Inc.
Printed and bound by Thomson-Shore, Inc.
The paper in this book meets the guidelines for
permanence and durability of the Committee on
Production Guidelines for Book Longevity of the
Council on Library Resources.

Most University of Georgia Press titles are
available from popular e-book vendors.

Printed in the United States of America
14 15 16 17 18 C 5 4 3 2 1

Library of Congress Cataloging-in-Publication Data

Moore, Deborah Dash, 1946–
Urban origins of American Judaism / Deborah Dash Moore. — First edition.
pages cm. — (George H. Shriver lecture series in
religion in American history ; number 6)
Includes bibliographical references and index.
ISBN-13: 978-0-8203-4682-3 (hardcover : alk. paper)
ISBN-10: 0-8203-4682-9 (hardcover : alk. paper)
1. Judaism—United States—History. I. Title.
BM205.M66 2014
296.0973—dc23
2014002328

British Library Cataloging-in-Publication Data available

IN MEMORY OF TWO CITY GIRLS

WHO BECAME

EXTRAORDINARY JEWISH WOMEN:

Pamela Ween Brumberg (1942–2002)

AND

Paula E. Hyman (1945–2011)

CONTENTS

ILLUSTRATIONS

FOREWORD

The substance of the chapters of this book composed a series of lectures delivered by Dr. Deborah Dash Moore at Stetson University in February 2012 as a part of the George H. Shriver Lectures: Religion in American History. The Shriver Lectures, inaugurated in 2000, were established through the generosity of a Stetson alumnus, Dr. George H. Shriver, professor of history emeritus at Georgia Southern University. The focus of the Shriver Lectures combines two of Dr. Shriver's academic passions—history and religious studies. The 2012 Shriver Lectures were the seventh set of lectures in the series. Previous lecturers and their topics were as follows:

2000. John F. Wilson, Religion in America: Historiography and History
2002. Martin E. Marty, American Religion: From Protestant through Pluralist to Public
2004. Yvonne Y. Haddad, The American Encounter with Islam
2006. Edward J. Larson, Historical Perspectives on the Ongoing Creation-Evolution Debate
2008. David L. Holmes, Religious but Usually Not Too Religious: The Faiths of the Post–World War II Presidents
2010. James Turner, The Study of Religions in America: The Early Years

The 2012 Shriver Lectures were delivered by Deborah Dash Moore, who is Frederick G. L. Huetwell Professor of History at the University of Michigan and director of the Jean and Samuel Frankel Center for Judaic

Studies. A specialist in twentieth-century American Jewish history, she is the author of several works, including *At Home in America: Second Generation New York Jews* (1981), *To the Golden Cities: Pursuing the American Jewish Dream in Miami and L.A.* (1994), *B'nai B'rith and the Challenge of Ethnic Leadership* (1981), and *GI Jews: How World War II Changed a Generation* (2004), and editor of *American Jewish Identity Politics* (2008).

Professor Moore's study examines the origin and development of Judaism in urban America, exploring the ways in which American cities both shaped and were themselves shaped by the vibrant Jewish communities that made them their home. Through a focus on synagogues, streets, and photographs, Moore demonstrates that American Judaism is rooted in city life, and particularly the experiences of large cities. Professor Moore's work is a fascinating and valuable contribution to our understanding of the importance of Judaism as a part of the American cultural and religious landscape. Her lectures fulfill admirably the intention of the Shriver Lecture Series, which is to explore, elucidate, and analyze the role of religion in America's history.

Special thanks must be extended to Professor Moore for her generosity in sharing her time and her insights through her spoken words on the Stetson campus and now through these printed words. I also wish once more to express deepest gratitude to George Shriver, whose benevolence made these lectures possible. Lisa Guenther, administrative specialist in the Department of Religious Studies, expertly handled all the small details that were necessary for the lectures to occur. Appreciation is also expressed to the people at the University of Georgia Press for their skillful publication of all the works in this series.

Mitchell G. Reddish, Chair
George H. Shriver Lectures Committee
Stetson University

PREFACE

Jews have lived in cities for many centuries. Scholars of Talmud, of medieval walled cities, and of Mediterranean cities often point to the influence on Jewish religious practices of diversity and pluralism in cities, as well as their economic and political structures. Yet Jews also possessed a long tradition of town dwelling from North Africa to Poland. There they fashioned a way of life based on the intimacies of knowing one's neighbors' business. Urbanization and industrialization in the eighteenth and nineteenth centuries drew Jews to large cities where they participated in shaping modern urban culture, in the process transforming Judaism.

Jewish migration to the United States occurred mostly in the nineteenth and twentieth centuries, when new American cities were growing rapidly. Although some Jews ignored the dominant trend toward urbanization, most enthusiastically joined in building American cities. Metropolitan development modified Judaism as Jews adapted to American society and culture. Rural traditions, New England small-town customs, plantation slavery, western ranching and farming practices exerted little impact on Jews as they became Americans.

This book argues that what we know today as American Judaism emerged out of Jewish encounters with American cities. Jews used the urban milieu to express themselves as Jews and as Americans. The demands of living and earning a livelihood in crowded cities in the nineteenth and twentieth centuries encouraged Jews to adjust their religious practices. These adjustments formed the origins of American Judaism.

Books often grow out of conversations, as was the case with *Urban Origins of American Judaism*. Almost a decade ago when Michael Alexander was directing the Myer and Rosalie Feinstein Center for American Jewish History at Temple University, he approached me with the idea of a lecture series and we talked about the theme of Jews and the city. Then the Frankel Institute for Advanced Judaic Studies devoted 2007–8 to that theme. At weekly workshops I learned to think about Jewish experience in American cities in comparison with ancient, medieval, modern European and North African cities, as well as contemporary Israeli cities.

When Mitchell Reddish invited me to give three lectures at Stetson University in 2011, he encouraged me to focus on urban religious life. I had taught several courses on urban religion in the United States, which influenced my lectures. Conversation with Riv-Ellen Prell of the University of Minnesota subsequently sharpened and refined my thinking.

I am grateful to these interlocutors for the pleasures of conversation, especially the rewards of contemplating Judaism as an urban religion in the United States. Their questions spurred me to clarify initially nebulous concepts and to locate an arc of historical development that distinguishes American Judaism from other contemporary formations.

Research inevitably involves collaboration, and I appreciate the archivists and librarians who have helped to make this book possible. Many of the following pages draw upon my research for articles published over a span of several decades. I am grateful to the publishers, Brandeis University Press, Indiana University Press, Russell Sage Foundation, and University of South Carolina Press, and to the editors of these volumes, Hasia Diner, Marion Kaplan, Dale and Ted Rosengarten, Jeffrey Shandler, David Ward, Beth S. Wenger, Jack Wertheimer, and Olivier Zunz, for permission to use these articles. Several University of Michigan students helped me. Joseph Eskin did excellent research and Shayna Goodman provided valued assistance preparing the manuscript for publication. In addition, Noa Gutterman contributed research over the course of a summer internship. The University of Michigan provided financial resources to defray some of the costs of acquiring permissions for images. I am fortunate to have received such aid.

At the University of Georgia Press an excellent staff handled publication, beginning with Editor-in-Chief Mick Gusinde-Duffy and Acquisitions Editor Beth Snead; David Des Jardines handled promotion, and Jon Davies oversaw the production process. Joseph A. Dahm improved the manuscript by catching my errors; I am grateful for his careful editing. Needless to say, I remain responsible for the book.

Two dear friends and colleagues read the manuscript in its entirety. I am enormously indebted to Andrew Bush of Vassar College and Riv-Ellen Prell for their insightful comments that enriched the book and for their refusal to let slide sloppy thinking and careless writing. Andy's enthusiastic willingness to read helped me finish the manuscript so that I would not disappoint him. Ever generous with his time and insight, my husband MacDonald Moore helped me at numerous junctures, especially with the third chapter, on photography. I could never have completed this book without his love and support.

Leaving New York City for Ann Arbor contributed another perspective. As we returned regularly to visit our family, I observed city living for the first time in part as an outsider. I watched our grandchildren—Elijah, Zoe, and Rose—grow up and my parents, Irene and Martin Dash, grow older in the city. I saw how cities shaped Jewish lives. The unstinting love and support of my city family, especially Mordecai and Mikhael, and their partners, Lori Moore and Deborah Axt, have made writing this book possible.

This is the first book I am publishing without the wise comments of two dear friends. To say that I miss them is an understatement. Both Paula Hyman and Pamela Brumberg loved cities. Not only did they grow up in them (Paula in Boston and Pamela in New York), but they also lived most of their lives in cities (Paula in New York and New Haven, and Pamela in New York). I would like to think that they would have appreciated this book. It is with a mix of grief and love that I dedicate this book to their memory.

Deborah Dash Moore
Ann Arbor, 2013

URBAN ORIGINS OF AMERICAN JUDAISM

INTRODUCTION

Looking back over several centuries, American Jewish historians point to a number of central themes. They see both migration and freedom as keys to understanding American Judaism. After all, as Jews came to U.S. shores from abroad, some immediately picked up and moved inland to seek their fortunes, attesting to the influence of migrations. But Jews also enjoyed opportunities for reinvention and renewal nurtured by a country that effectively promoted a free marketplace of religions, new and old. Hence freedom. To complicate matters further, scholars debate the significance of American Judaism and its place within the longue durée of Jewish history seeking to explain how Jewish life adapted through years of disruptions, dispersions, and resettlements across Europe, the Mediterranean, and the Americas. Historians have also emphasized connections with Judaism as it developed elsewhere, including such important trends as the rise of religious reform in the nineteenth century. With such a complicated past, Jews often find reassurance in perceived continuities across time and space. Continuities do exist across generations and continents, but like life itself they are dynamic, not static.

This volume takes a different approach, contending that critical features of American Judaism can be understood as an imaginative product grounded in urban potentials. While not denying the importance of ties to an Old World past or transnational Jewish present, it posits the formative power of city living on American Jews as they fashioned intertwined forms of religious and material life.

More so than many American religious groups, Jews cast their lot with American cities. For roughly two centuries, and to a lesser degree after extensive suburbanization occurred following World War II, Jews made their homes in some of the nation's largest and most dynamic cities. Jews saw in urban space opportunities both to preserve traditions and to devise new patterns of living. Many American Jews sought to transform selected segments of the urban grid into recognizable Jewish places, putting a distinctive stamp on city streets, commerce, and culture. Thus urbanism as an aspect of Jewish life emerged as one of American Judaism's distinctive features.[1] These changes occurred even as European Jews were migrating to rapidly growing cities in record numbers, producing parallel developments on both sides of the Atlantic. But unlike the experiences of their cousins in Europe, where urban life "ate away at Jewish religious life," American Jews discovered unparalleled opportunities for religious creativity in cities.[2] The United States lacked the rural backcountry Jewish experience to compare and interact with the urban one. From a New World perspective, both city and town (*shtetl*) were equally part of the Old World. In the United States, urban attitudes and assumptions became embedded in Jewish religious institutions, practices, and beliefs. Even after Jews moved to the suburbs, their American Judaism retained associational patterns and a commitment to pluralism associated with urbanism.

Rooted in city streets, American Judaism took shape in response to encounters with density, diversity, economic innovation, and cultural productivity that characterized American urban milieus. Both continuities and innovations emerged as a result. Of course the United States includes many different types of cities, not all of them particularly attractive to Jews. The largest, most dynamic urban hubs served as primary sites of Jewish settlement and community. As those cities changed and grew, so did Jewish religious activities. Over the course of three centuries—as colonial seaports grew into industrial metropolises—urban economies, politics, and cultures nurtured Jewish social, cultural, political, and religious behaviors that meshed well with changing American practices.

Jews discovered many ways to be Jewish in an urban milieu. Cities fostered continuities of religious and ethnic sentiments and ways of living, integrating variability into the fabric of Jewish religious life at the same time as they provided spaces for experimentation. Some innovations emerged as a result of ideology and theology; others appeared in response to living in densely populated capitalist milieus. Jews enjoyed opportunities to feel Jewish in urban enclaves just from seeing synagogues in local neighborhoods. Walking by synagogues, even for those who never entered them, transformed them into features of the cityscape that signaled a Jewish presence, permitting Jews a measure of ethnic self-confidence in many cities. Jews were thus able to make a place for Judaism in the urban environment. Although it was always a minority religion in the United States, and often the only non-Christian religion in town, Judaism found a welcome measure of religious legitimacy in American cities.

Despite the Puritans' exaltation of the "city on the hill" as a model of Christian redemption, many Americans scorned cities as places of corruption and sin. They associated promiscuity with cities; the urban world's mixture of peoples and races, genders and sexual orientations, workers and wealthy provoked fear and disdain. In truth, cities encouraged novel forms of religious experience even as they allowed many residents to live in ways untouched by faith. Most important, cities allowed diverse minority groups to elaborate their own subcultures by affording them enough space. Ironically, despite chronic urban overcrowding, high rates of density, and occasionally bitter competition for scarce resources—especially living space—cities promoted productive interactive exchanges among immigrant groups as well as generating conflicts that often heightened awareness of class and racial differences. Jews participated in such shifting urban dynamics, unaware at times how they were integrating their religious lives into a city's multiethnic and multireligious society. Nor did Jews anticipate that these changes would recast American Judaism into a multiplicity that reflected salient features of their urban setting.

In the colonial era Jews crafted a religious way of life in five towns—Newport, New York, Charleston, Savannah, and Philadelphia—that took account of their social, political, economic, and cultural patterns. As seaports structured around trade across the Atlantic with mixed religious, ethnic, and racial populations, these towns permitted Jews not only to earn a livelihood but also to observe their religious commitments. As cities expanded rapidly in the early Republic, Jews adjusted their Judaism to reflect a newly popular democratic ethos that emerged with the mobilization of laborers and artisans during the American Revolution. With enthusiasm Jews wrote constitutions to govern their congregations. Democracy as it appeared on city streets appealed to them, and Jews incorporated its egalitarian principles into their collective life, even though that often meant struggling with fragmentation, class conflict, and ethnic diversity. Mass migration to the United States transformed American urbanism in the nineteenth century. Migrants founded new cities throughout the United States. These booming entrepôts of enterprise and exploitation exacerbated contrasts between rich and poor. Jews experienced all these changes. They participated in establishing new cities and expanding older ones. Thousands endured desperate poverty, and a handful tasted unimagined prosperity.[3]

During the first half of the twentieth century, Jews concentrated in such numbers in the largest cities of the United States that they often came to identify with them, especially the top two: New York and Chicago. So many Jews lived in New York prior to World War II that they constituted its largest single ethnic group. With roughly two million Jews at its peak, New York exerted enormous influence on the course of U.S. Jewish religious life.[4] After World War II, Jews joined the postwar migrations that transformed Los Angeles into the nation's second city, displacing Chicago. Los Angeles became their second city as well. But large numbers of Jews also moved south to such cities as Miami and then, in the final decades of the twentieth century, to Atlanta. In these multiethnic and multireligious cities, Jews and others worked to transform an intractable urban environment to build communities. The imprint of a new progressive, liberal urbanism registered on American Judaism in part because Jews helped to articulate an expansive political vision of what cities could and should do for their residents.

Concentration itself has implications for urban Judaism. In the United States, as in other parts of the Jewish diaspora, Jews chose to live near other Jews. Religious requirements for Sabbath observance mandated living within walking distance of a congregation. When that congregation existed in a city, Jews needed to navigate demands of urban life—including its density, extremes of poverty and wealth, occupational structures, pace, and dynamism—and adjust their Judaism. Those adjustments often included discarding many patterns of religious practice.

Yet until the 1970s most Jews preferred residences in cities to those in small towns, rural areas, and even suburbs. In the last decades of the twentieth century, like many Americans, Jews opted for suburban living, attenuating but not cutting their ties to cities. Despite such dispersion, many Americans rarely encounter Jews in their daily lives; most areas of the United States report no statistically significant number of Jews.[5]

There are other implications of concentration: around 2 percent of the American population is Jewish, but most Jews live in areas where they make up between 4 and 30 percent of the population. Thus Jews experience their lives as less of a minority than their numbers would suggest. Since most Jews live relatively close to other Jews, their concentration allows for diverse forms of Jewish religious expression to coexist, encouraging innovation and specialization along with pluralism. Political scientists note that concentration enhances Jewish political influence in large states.[6] Concentration also places Jews at centers of American cultural production since most media industries take root in cities.

This book explores Jewish participation in American cities and considers implications of urban living on Jews themselves. The urban origins of American Judaism begin with the experiences of Jews: their responses to opportunities for social and physical mobility that cities afforded them as well as to discrimination and prejudice encountered in those places. Jews signaled their collective presence in a city through synagogue construction. Synagogues represented Judaism on the civic stage, exemplifying public religious diversity and the inclusion of non-Christians in American urban society. In addition, such buildings expressed aesthetic aspirations and concretized Jewish spiritual desires. Their changing architecture reflected shifting values among American Jews, sometimes drawing attention through their exuberant design, while at other times gracefully merging into the cityscape. In either case, synagogues stood for an organized Jewish community, one committed to collective religious observance. The Jewish sacred calendar, both the weekly Saturday Sabbath and the annual cycle of holidays, could be observed in synagogues. Urban Jews also turned to synagogues not just for prayer but also to provide other elements of communal outreach—for example, the kosher slaughter of meat or the Hebrew lessons given to a boy in preparation for his bar mitzvah at age thirteen.

In the nineteenth century an increasing Jewish population in the United States generated vibrant street cultures that introduced additional urban dimensions to Judaism. Jewish religious practices marked nineteenth- and twentieth-century American city streets, contributing to a pluralist and multicultural ethos. Evidence of a Jewish urban presence existed in commerce seen in specialty stores—bakeries, butcher shops, delicatessens, and even cafés—that catered to Jewish requirements for kosher food as well as in burgeoning food industries that supplied those items. Rhythms of the Jewish calendar echoed on city streets. In Jewish neighborhoods commerce ground to a halt as Jews paused each fall to observe the high holy days signaling the beginning of the New Year followed ten days later by the Day of Atonement. Flimsy booths appeared shortly thereafter on the sidewalks, rooftops, and backyards of Jewish neighborhoods to celebrate the thanksgiving festival of Sukkot. And in the springtime, sanitation workers pulled extra shifts to handle the extensive housecleaning Jews pursued in the weeks before the Passover festival.

Jews also took their politics into the streets. Their marches in protest of Jewish persecution abroad stopped traffic, as did parades to celebrate the establishment of Israel in 1948. Massive funeral processions honoring a beloved political or cultural figure expressed commitments to socialism or Zionism. These "rites of community" identified shared Jewish concerns and inspired urban Jews to recommit themselves to collective action.[7]

Jewish and Christian observers often marveled that such experiences unfolded conspicuously, in public. These events and practices pervade photographs that recorded the texture of urban living and accounts told about Jews, not to mention stories Jews told about themselves. Such tales of neighborhood life evoked urban Judaism, picturing an energetic, aspiring, contentious cluster of immigrants and their children at home on the streets of American cities. Memoirs of growing up in tough urban enclaves interpreted Jewish city life for a wide audience. Both types of narratives, about Jews or by Jews, whether embedded in photos or recounted in texts, particularly appealed to Jews seeking a way to understand their past and forge connections to it. Even after massive migration to the suburbs transformed American Jewish life in the decades after World War II, cities retained their imaginative position as sites of authentic Jewishness, places where American Jews developed distinctive behaviors that defined Judaism as fundamentally diverse, open, eclectic, and vibrant.

This volume explores the urban origins of American Judaism across three centuries, investigating synagogues, streets, and snapshots. All three are sites of Jewish religious activity. Synagogues display Judaism in action, its rituals, liturgies, and community. But synagogues also demonstrate how Jews Judaized other aspects of their collective life, including study, education, recreation, sociability, and politics. Streets amplified an urban Jewish presence and provided vital contexts for synagogue life. Concentrations of Jews in cities allowed for development of public religious practices that ranged from weekly shopping for the Sabbath to exuberant dancing in the streets with Torah scrolls on the holiday of Simhat Torah. Jewish engagement with city streets reflected as well Jewish responses to Irish and Italian Catholic religious practices that temporarily transformed streets into sacred spaces. An urban Judaism had to compete with the city's daily spectacles, had to provide quotidian solace and sustenance in addition to transformative transcendence and solidarity. Jewish life necessarily adjusted to the rich and enticing commercial entertainments available. Jews repeatedly devised new ways to make their urban Judaism compelling. Although Jews only occasionally imagined their cities as American versions of the heavenly and earthly city of Jerusalem, they did put into pictures and stories their intense and rich urban Judaism, employing snapshots to freeze a moment in time to be savored in the present. These visual and oral narratives conveyed to future generations, especially suburbanites, powerful experiences of Jewish urban life.

CHAPTER 1

SYNAGOGUES

Synagogues announced a Jewish presence in a city. While they represent the most visible manifestation of Judaism, their changing architecture articulates shifting visions of Jewish religious practice and Jewish understandings of American urbanism. American cities left their imprint on Jews that registered in the very structure of their synagogues as well as the scope of activities associated with them. Synagogues came to reflect varied versions of Judaism, both in their exterior presence and, even more, in their interiors. Looking at synagogues across three centuries provides a window into Jewish religious life, as congregations became the fundamental voluntary unit of Judaism in America. But synagogues also implicitly comment on American urbanism's aspirations and politics, since Jews desired to secure a place for Judaism in American society.

Jews did not need a synagogue for community prayer. Both private prayer and collective prayer could and did occur within a home, at the back of a store, or even in lodge meeting rooms. A decision not only to establish a congregation but also to house it within a synagogue represented a serious commitment on the part of Jews to participate as Jews in urban life. While not all congregations possessed synagogues, many did. Without a formal, legally recognized Jewish community and a nationally established chief rabbinate, or even a chief rabbi for individual cities and towns as existed in Europe, North Africa, and the Middle East, American Jews made do with congregational forms of religious organization that lodged authority in prosperous male lay leaders who possessed the power to hire—and fire—rabbis and other religious functionaries, such as cantors.[1]

Small numbers of Jews settled in five Atlantic seaports during the colonial era: New York, Charleston, Newport, Savannah, and Philadelphia. In each of these cities lived only a few hundred Jews; most engaged in trade, either local or overseas, as merchants or worked in crafts. The most prosperous Jews participated in an Atlantic commercial network that connected London and Amsterdam with Surinam, Curaçao, Jamaica, and other ports in the West Indies.[2]

Despite their small numbers, colonial Jews all built synagogues during the eighteenth century as expressions of their urban prosperity and willingness to establish roots. Since Jews need only a quorum of ten men (a *minyan*) to conduct regular worship three times a day, establishing a congregation indicated Jews' desires for community as well as prayer. As a formally organized religious unit, a Jewish congregation stood for more than the sum of its members; it represented another link in the long chain of autonomous Jewish community (the *kehillah*) history. Furthermore, since communal prayer occurred in private homes, especially once a congregation possessed a Torah scroll, embarking on a project to construct a special synagogue building or purchasing a building to be used primarily as a synagogue and sanctifying its space reflected commitment and security as well as pride and permanence on the part of Jews.

Colonial synagogues revealed Jewish identification with the American city externally and reserved their sense of difference from Christian Americans for the inside. The buildings themselves implied the multireligious character of these towns. Synagogues acknowledged a Jewish urban presence and invited Christians to reflect on their own faith and willingness to accommodate non-Christian believers. Indeed, colonial seaports unwilling to welcome non-Christians (such as Boston) did not house synagogues and their few Jewish residents worshipped in private.[3]

Although only one of these colonial synagogues survives today—in Newport, Rhode Island, now a city with relatively few Jews—its architecture exemplifies an eighteenth-century Jewish way of being both urban and American. Ironically, its preservation derives in part from its abandonment in the early nineteenth century, which stimulated Judah Touro, a prosperous and generous New Orleans Jewish philanthropist, to save it. Renamed the Touro Synagogue in his honor, it captures a moment in American Judaism when Jews lived as a miniscule non-Christian minority integrated into colonial urban society. It reminds us, too, that abandonment as much as construction of synagogues characterized Jewish city experiences. Impulses for preservation and restoration similarly appear very early in American Jewish history. Transformation of a synagogue into a museum or a National Historic Site, as is the case with Touro Synagogue, invites outsiders to enter and temporarily become insiders, instructed in Jewish religious practices.

Designed by a famous colonial architect, Peter Harrison, the building's modest exterior shares much in common with New England churches in its simplicity. Knowing eyes would have missed a steeple that defined Christian churches, but the plain white geometry blends unassumingly into Newport's urban fabric. The building appears to be a large, private white house. Jews considered a synagogue a place to gather (*Bet Knesset*) as well as a place of prayer, so architecture that reflected residential models would have made sense to them. From a Christian perspective, however, the synagogue's domestic aspects probably enhanced

Touro Synagogue, Newport, Rhode Island, oldest synagogue in the United States, 1763. Postcard, *Old Jewish Synagogue, Newport, Rhode Island*, ca. 1910. Courtesy Library of Congress, Hebraic Division.

its unobtrusive qualities; it would have been easier for them to tolerate Jewish religious practice in private settings. Yet inside the synagogue another world is revealed, reflecting Sephardic Jewish practice. Standing inside transports one into a culture defined in part by the expulsion of Jews from Spain (1492) and Portugal (1497) and their persecution by the Catholic Church.

Jews from the Iberian Peninsula—Sephardi Jews—developed distinctive religious practices and transplanted them throughout the Mediterranean and among port cities, including Amsterdam. Many of the first Jews to settle in the British colonies of North America were of Sephardi background, and they established the conduct of congregational organization and prayer. Sephardi Jews often knew Ladino (a Jewish language based on Spanish but written in Hebrew letters), and many possessed great familiarity with Christianity because they had lived as Catholics before feeling free enough to return to Jewish observance. Sephardic practice structured a synagogue's internal space by placing the ark containing the Torah scrolls on the eastern wall facing Jerusalem and the *bima*, the platform where the Torah scroll was read, close to the western wall. This placement invited a long walk from ark to bima with the scrolls each Sabbath and holy day when the sacred scriptures were read, allowing congregants to feel the spiritual presence of God's words on the Torah scrolls.

Women watched from the balcony. Jewish women traditionally sat apart from men during prayer, and a separate floor for women was an interpretation of the *mechitza* or barrier designed to separate women from men. Colonial Jews adopted the practice of placing the women's section in a balcony, drawing on its prominence in the magnificent seventeenth-century Sephardic synagogue in Amsterdam. Women could observe worship services and could pray at their own pace but could neither lead public prayer nor read from the Torah scroll. Christian visitors would have noted the absence of both music and images as well as the segregation of women as distinctive Jewish practices, along with prayer in Hebrew and white prayer shawls (*tallit*) worn by men as well as their custom of covering their heads.[4]

Colonial synagogues expressed the modesty of colonial Jews. They lacked the grandeur of Amsterdam's seventeenth-century Spanish and

Interior of Touro Synagogue, Newport, Rhode Island, showing *bima* for reading the Torah scrolls, chandeliers, and balcony. © Touro Synagogue Foundation / John Hopf.

Portuguese synagogue that towered above its surrounding buildings. Nor did they approach London's Bevis Marks Synagogue, whose plain exterior integrated the building into the street façade but whose interior was modeled on that of Amsterdam. They did not resemble the massive wooden synagogues of Polish Jews situated in small towns or the cramped ghetto synagogues of Italy, often located on upper floors in ordinary buildings. Their modesty reflected not only the small numbers of Jews in colonial seaports but also the adherents' relatively restricted financial means. These colonial synagogues did not stand adjacent to other buildings for designated Jewish communal uses—such as the study hall or the ritual bath—as was common in Eastern Europe. Rather, colonial synagogues stood alone in the city, assuming prominence as the focal point of Jewish communal life. Jewish congregations accepted responsibility for many elements of Jewish religious practice, including kosher slaughter of animals for food, primary education of children, and assistance to the poor, orphaned, sick, and widowed.[5]

By the time the poet Emma Lazarus, who would acquire renown for her verses inscribed on the Statue of Liberty, visited Newport's synagogue and signed its guest register, three days before her eighteenth birthday in July 1867, the previously abandoned synagogue had been partially revived. Newport's growing popularity among wealthy Christians and Jews as a fashionable place to spend summers led to the synagogue's reopening for visits during those months. Lazarus, born into a prosperous Sephardic Jewish family in New York City in 1849, had relatives who had worshipped in the Newport synagogue in the previous century. A precocious and talented young poet, she had already published a slim volume of poetry sponsored by her father. Later that year she corresponded with Ralph Waldo Emerson, a leading American intellectual of the period. Her early poetry expressed romantic and Victorian sensibilities. "In the Jewish Synagogue at Newport," written after her visit, suggests a somewhat different perspective, although her elegiac stance is a romantic trope that also works to claim a history for herself as an alienated modern.[6]

> Here, where the noises of the busy town,
> The ocean's plunge and roar can enter not,
> We stand and gaze around with tearful awe,
> And muse upon the consecrated spot.
>
> No signs of life are here: the very prayers
> Inscribed around are in a language dead;
> The light of the "perpetual lamp" is spent
> That an undying radiance was to shed.

Lazarus muses on the brilliance of the Jewish past and the pain of exile. The "Eternal Light" that hangs in front of the ark that houses the sacred Torah scrolls in all synagogues has gone dark because no congregants gather to pray. The physical space of the synagogue invites her contemplation of Jewish tradition. She imagines that Hebrew, the sacred tongue, has also died. In her poem she contemplates the long course of Jewish history connecting Newport back over thousands of years to the ancient Israelites and forward to her American self and her family. She concludes,

> Nathless the sacred shrine is holy yet,
> With its lone floors where reverent feet once trod.
> Take off your shoes as by the burning bush,
> Before the mystery of death and God.[7]

The abandoned synagogue still inspires reverence and bears a transcendent message, "an intense awe for a human source of holiness."[8] God's mystery is revealed not in the eternal "perpetual lamp" but rather as guarantor of meaning in the face of passing time.

Esther Schor, Lazarus's biographer, argues that her poem signals her "willingness—her eagerness—to cross the gulf between her own assimilated modern American life and the ancient tradition of Judaism and its people."[9] Rather than writing about a yearning for Zion, Lazarus visits the Touro Synagogue and grounds modernity in the history of a specific American Jewish place.[10] In the twentieth century other Jews would follow in Lazarus's footsteps, revisiting abandoned synagogues. These Jews, too, would seek to hear the synagogue's historic religious message and bridge the gap between their modern American lives and Judaism's ancient traditions. By rescuing and restoring failing urban synagogues, a handful of American Jews would accept responsibility to reinterpret them for a contemporary world.[11]

Early North American synagogues expressed the first stirrings of freedom of religion as it took shape in Britain's American colonies. Newport's synagogue was dedicated in 1763, over a century after the first Jews came to the town. It enjoyed only little more than a decade of use before the British army occupied Newport during the Revolutionary War, prompting most Jews to flee to Connecticut. With the end of the war, they returned to Newport and their synagogue.

In 1790, when George Washington visited the city, Moses Seixas, president of the synagogue and Emma Lazarus's relative, welcomed him on behalf of the congregation. Seixas characterized the new American Constitution as "a Government which to bigotry gives no sanction, to persecution no assistance—but generously affording to All liberty of conscience, and immunities of citizenship: deeming every one, of whatever nation, tongue or language equal parts of the great Governmental Machine." Washington echoed Seixas in his reply. "All possess alike liberty of conscience and immunities of citizenship," Washington wrote. "It is now no more that toleration is spoken of, as if it was by the indulgence of one class of people that another enjoyed the exercise of their inherent natural rights. For happily the Government of the United States, which gives to bigotry no sanction, to persecution no assistance, requires only that they who live under its protection, should demean themselves as good citizens." Thus Washington sanctioned Seixas's phrase "to bigotry no sanction, to persecution no assistance" as part of an emerging American creed associated with the new nation. But he embellished it, expressing his wish that each of the "children of the Stock of Abraham" should "sit in safety under his own vine and figtree, and there shall be none to make him afraid" (Micah 4:4).[12] Washington's addition extended a promise of a life without fear, something that American Jews would fight to achieve and come to cherish in future decades.[13]

Moses Seixas's letter on behalf of the congregation not only reflected sincere desires but also strategically sought the first president's support for religious freedom. Since Jews were not guaranteed all the rights of citizenship in Rhode Island at this time, they looked to the new federal government for a model of equal citizenship. In this they were not disappointed. The Constitution proscribed a religious oath for holding office, allowing Jews elected to Congress to be sworn in as federal lawmakers. The First Amendment in the new Bill of Rights guaranteed that Congress "shall make no law respecting an establishment of religion, or prohibiting the free exercise thereof." It would take several decades before the federal model led states to change their laws, but by 1868 the last of state political restrictions on Jews had been removed.[14]

Jews were developing urban religious forms responsive to their new political situation in North America, where they possessed citizenship and political rights. In Charleston, South Carolina, the city with the largest Jewish population in the colonies by the end of the eighteenth century, with an estimated population of six hundred, Jews formed close to 5 percent of the white population, itself a minority in this southern city. Although they lived scattered in various parts of Charleston, many Jews located their businesses on King Street, the emotional if not geographical center of the city for Jews. Members of the city's only congregation, Kahal Kadosh Beth Elohim (KKBE: Holy Congregation House of God), expressed their understanding of America's democratic pluralism in a new synagogue building they constructed in 1794 on Hasell Street.

The synagogue's exterior, modeled on that of St. Michael's Episcopal Church, one of the city's foremost churches, proclaimed Charleston Jews' sense of place as well as their willingness to borrow styles of

Christian architecture. Blending into Charleston, a slaveholding city with an Episcopalian elite, required different architecture than in Newport. Unlike the Newport synagogue, KKBE possessed a spire, visible on the skyline but not overreaching. It symbolized the congregation's "aspirations to full integration into the city's civic and religious life."[15] Charleston Jews identified through their architecture with the republican slave-owning city and accepted a design demonstrating that Judaism participated in the town's public culture.

If the exterior spoke to one type of religious pluralism, its interior addressed different concerns. Many of KKBE's members came from Ashkenazi European backgrounds. They hailed from German lands and often spoke Yiddish. Yet they wanted Jewish visitors, especially merchants of Sephardi backgrounds with whom they traded, to feel comfortable in their synagogue. Ashkenazi congregations usually placed the reading platform (bima) in the center of the synagogue, physically centering the reading of the Torah, rather than near the western wall. So Charleston Jews split the difference between two Jewish practices, placing the bima not quite in the middle but not at the end. This compromise represented an early effort at Jewish accommodation spurred in part by seaport trading realities.[16]

Charleston Jews integrated themselves into white urban society even as they maintained religious separation. They acquired several burial grounds, started a Hebrew Benevolent Society (1784) to provide assistance to the poor, widows, and orphans, and in 1801 established the first Hebrew Orphan Society in the United States.[17] The latter, an urban innovation, exemplified how Jews learned from Christians when they not only shared city streets but also joined together in organizations designed to improve city living. Jews and Christians met socially as members of the Masonic Temple and in a handful of literary groups that bridged the city's class and denominational lines. Jews nonetheless maintained their religious differences. Charleston Jews constructed both a *mikva* (ritual bath) and a communal oven to bake *matzah* (unleavened bread) for Passover. Married women needed the former for purification after their menstrual cycle so that they could resume sexual relations with their husbands.

A native-born generation was growing up in the city. These American Jews spoke English, cherished their political rights as white men, condoned and justified slavery, and aspired to contribute to society. By 1830, 83 percent of Charleston's Jews owned slaves, slightly fewer than the 87 percent of all whites who were slave owners. Jews participated in buying and selling chattel slaves and articulated no critique of slavery, based on either Jewish historical experience or theology. The state's 1790 constitution guaranteed the free exercise of religion, and Jews took part in elections, even running for office. Their slaveholding, as much as their office holding, signified their assimilation into Charleston society and culture. In 1812, when Governor Henry Middleton proclaimed a day of Thanksgiving to be observed by the state's churches, Charleston's KKBE objected to his exclusion of Jews. The governor's admission of his oversight reinforced Jews' understanding of their religious rights. It also emboldened Jews to think of themselves as secure citizens.[18]

At this transitional moment for Charleston and its Jews, architecture and urbanism, politics and religion molded a new Republican form of American Judaism. But rather than a synthesis of innovative orphan asylum and traditional mikva, the unity of congregation and community started to fracture. Soon a younger leadership gravitated around the Hebrew Orphan Asylum, while older men controlled the synagogue. In 1824 these native-born Jews petitioned the city's only Jewish congregation for change. They were fomenting their own revolution. Borrowing language of political reform articulated by those seeking urban improvements to prevent Charleston from losing its prominence as a seaport, young Jewish men claimed to see the same "apathy and neglect" manifested toward "our holy religion" as the town fathers saw in the city itself. These impatient "inheritors of the *true faith*" sought to solve the riddle of their own lack of interest in the synagogue.[19] The problem, they concluded, lay in the congregation's worship services.[20]

In attempting to reform Jewish prayer, the petitioners were expressing similar ambitions as their German Jewish contemporaries in Hamburg and Berlin. Reform was in the air in the early nineteenth century on both sides of the Atlantic.

The Charleston reformers proposed a "more rational means of worshipping the true God" as a solution for themselves and their children. This meant in practical terms that services should include English as well as Hebrew so that worshippers could understand the prayers. A sermon on the weekly Torah portion would similarly advance a native-born generation's comprehension. Shorter services and more decorum—eliminating the auctioning of honors to read the Torah would produce both—would elicit respect from their white Christian neighbors. The petitioners specifically mentioned Roman Catholicism, Lutheranism, and French Protestantism, all minority faiths in a city with an Episcopalian elite and growing numbers of Baptists and Methodists. Desire for decorum also expressed Jewish aspirations for bourgeois respectability. Jews traditionally prayed aloud at their own pace (and if they arrived late they did not skip to catch up but said all the prayers very quickly). This style of worship produced a measure of cacophony in a congregation, although usually congregants pronounced in unison certain key prayers. They also remained on the same page for the section of the service devoted to reading the Torah. The petitioners, however, anticipated what would subsequently become a trend. "They wanted their synagogues to be compatible with the aesthetics associated with American Protestant life," argues anthropologist Riv-Ellen Prell. "They also wanted to create a synagogue that accepted their inconsistent practice of Judaism."[21]

Aware of the inroads of evangelism, including missions to convert the Jews, the dissidents appealed for "outreach" to Jews and gentiles alike to spread Judaism's sacred message. Mostly, undoubtedly, they had in mind themselves, since few were members of the congregation and three had intermarried, though all identified as Jews. "We wish not to *overthrow*, but to *rebuild*," they explained. "We wish not to *destroy*, but to *reform* . . . ; we wish not to *abandon* the institutions of Moses, but to *understand* and *observe them*." Then, in a concluding stab, the men wrote that they "wish to worship God, not as *slaves of bigotry and priestcraft*, but as the enlightened descendants of that chosen race."[22] The metaphor of slavery surely raised hackles among the congregation's leadership, who did not identify with their black slaves and would have resented a comparison of traditional Jewish religious worship with slavery.

Perhaps not unexpectedly, KKBE's leaders rejected the petition. Older than the petitioners, well established, with high status based on their wealth, they were not inclined to entertain suggestions for upsetting the status quo from men young enough to be their sons. In fact, several of them were their sons.

Revolutionary ideas influenced how Jews thought about themselves as Americans and Jews. The Constitution and Bill of Rights' articulation of separation of church and state as well as religious freedom stimulated Jews to embrace democracy in their religious lives. "Already in the late colonial period," writes historian Jonathan Sarna, "American Judaism had begun to diverge from religious patterns that existed in Europe and the Caribbean. The American Revolution, the ratification of the Constitution, the passage of the Bill of Rights, and the nationwide democratization of religion that followed from these developments further transformed Jewish religious life." These democratic trends, abetted by increasing numbers of Jewish immigrants arriving in America's port cities, inspired Jews to introduce religious innovation and pluralism into their urban Judaism. Sarna argues that the shift in the 1820s from a unified "synagogue community" to a pluralistic "community of synagogues" proved to be the "first dramatic turning point in the history of American Judaism."[23]

The Charleston petition highlighted the urban genesis of Reform Judaism. Opportunities the city offered for alternative forms of Jewish community brought these young men together and encouraged them to imagine something different. They mixed with diverse white Protestants, occasionally attended their churches, and collaborated to fashion a lively urban culture that included theater and literature. Cosmopolitan Charleston even pushed them to consider their sisters as potentially equal members of the Jewish community. Yet without the establishment of the Hebrew Orphan Society and its many benefit activities designed to raise funds, the reformers would not have had an alternative organizational base in the city as a vantage point from which to contemplate what they thought was wrong with the synagogue. The reformers preferred to participate in Hebrew Orphan Society events rather than in synagogue services. Still, they implicitly recognized the synagogue's centrality to Jewish religious life and sought to refashion it to fit their needs. They could not ignore the synagogue.

KKBE's rejection of their petition galvanized the younger generation to organize the Reformed Society of Israelites. Initially modeled on similar societies formed by Baptists and Methodists in Charleston, the Jewish society in January 1825 began holding monthly meetings, consisting of a mix of cultural and social activities. Its constitution, adopted the following month, allowed any male Jew aged at least seventeen to join, thus eliminating KKBE's restrictions against those who intermarried. The society attracted a membership of approximately fifty men, who together with their families probably numbered two hundred—a significant minority of the city's Jews. By the end of the year, the society had incorporated, heading down the path of becoming another congregation.

After all, when Jews met together regularly, eager to reform their ancient religion, a desire to translate theory into practice would be hard to resist. (A century later in New York City a group of Jews created the Society for the Advancement of Judaism to promote the "reconstruction" of Jewish life, seeking, as did Charleston Jews, "to rebuild," and soon they, too, decided they might as well pray together as a congregation.) The Reformed Society started to hold Sabbath services at Seyle's Masonic Hall on Meeting Street. At services members prayed in English as well as Hebrew, read the Torah in both languages, enjoyed music from a choir and instruments, sang hymns, and listened to a sermon in English. This shortened service emphasized decorum and education. Apparently women also participated by joining the choir and writing hymns for the Sabbath.

In 1828 Abraham Moïse, a lawyer, ascended to the presidency of the society, a position he held until its demise roughly a decade later. Under his leadership, the society published its prayer book in 1830. Historian of Reform Judaism Michael Meyer calls its predecessor, a handwritten prayer book, "the first radical liturgy produced in the Reform movement anywhere," almost twenty years ahead of the 1845 prayer book compiled by the Berlin Reform Congregation.[24] The Reformed Society's prayer book included such innovations as an individual confirmation ritual that involved recitation of the society's revised version of Maimonides's articles of faith. This creed, reduced from thirteen statements of faith to ten—closer to both the Ten Commandments and the Bill of Rights—eliminated affirmation of a personal Messiah and belief in resurrection of the dead and substituted for them a rejection of the Christian Messiah and belief in immortality of the soul. Although modern and American, this new Jewish theology expressed hostility to Christianity, especially an increasingly prominent evangelizing Christian church.

Despite such a promising and ambitious beginning, the Reformed Society of Israelites folded after a decade. The enthusiasm that sustained the society for its first years waned as members left the city, died, or dropped out. KKBE's leaders maintained a steady barrage of criticism. Some young men, who might have been tempted to join the society, refrained out respect for their parents. Eventually, even Moïse admitted defeat. Unable to change Judaism through an independent society, he rejoined KKBE and discovered possibilities for reform from within. By helping to write a new constitution for the congregation in 1836, Moïse introduced some ideas advocated by the reformers. Most significant, KKBE decided that their religious leader should know both Hebrew and English and give a regular "Discourse" on the Sabbath. The congregation chose Gustavus Poznanski, an observant Polish Jewish immigrant educated in Germany, who worked as a *shohet* (a ritual slaughterer) in New York City, to fulfill these new responsibilities.

A fire that destroyed the old synagogue in 1838 set the stage for more changes. In the process of rebuilding, thirty-eight members petitioned for an organ. Traditional European Jewish synagogues did not have organs since playing an instrument was considered a desecration of Sabbath prohibitions against work. However, Poznanski supported the petitioners. A talented musician, he welcomed a chance to enhance worship services with music. Although the proposal was opposed by the leadership, a narrow majority of congregants favored it. A minority reacted to their defeat by withdrawing to form a separate, traditional congregation. Thus Charleston reformers also helped to shape orthodox traditionalists, who gained a sense of their own distinctive identity through their quarrel with reform.

The new synagogue building, with its organ, facilitated further innovations. Women's voices were heard. Abraham Moïse's sister, Penina Moïse, wrote a hymn for the synagogue dedication, and she was perhaps the first woman in American Judaism to contribute to synagogue liturgy. It would not be her only contribution. She subsequently composed sixty of the seventy-four songs for KKBE's hymnal, published in 1842.

Later, as Reform became a movement in American Judaism, other congregations adopted some of her hymns, and editors of the hymnal of the Union of American Hebrew Congregations (UAHC) included over a dozen of them. Several were set to music.[25]

Cities encouraged Jewish women to organize by giving them opportunities to meet and mingle with other Christian and Jewish women, to participate in varied institutional settings, and to channel their creative energies. In Philadelphia in 1818, Rebecca Gratz established the Female Hebrew Benevolent Society. Modeled on similar Christian societies for women in which she participated, it aimed to help indigent Jewish women and children. At the same time, however, Gratz sought to protect them from the importuning of evangelists seeking to convert vulnerable Jews. Largely excluded from the synagogue, pious Jewish women fashioned alternative forms of community to express their own beliefs. Gratz, a prominent and prosperous single woman profoundly devoted to Judaism, necessarily sought means of expressing her piety outside the synagogue's orbit. As an activist in Philadelphia women's circles, she avidly participated in emerging new republican reforms designed to improve American urban society. Twenty years later, Gratz adapted the concept of Christian Sunday schools and established weekly religious instruction for Jewish boys and girls with women teachers. This extraordinary innovation in Jewish practice—women had never served as religious instructors in Europe, North Africa, or the Middle East—soon spread to other American cities where Jews lived.[26]

American Jews' intimate contact in the years before the Civil War with middle-class Christian city dwellers who espoused diverse forms of Protestantism motivated Jews to experiment with associations and schools derived from Christian practices. American cities in the nineteenth century were expanding rapidly, leaving huge holes in the social fabric. Women often stepped in to mend those tears, helping the poor and needy, healing the sick, and educating children. Middle-class Jewish women joined their Christian counterparts in addressing the ills of urban life. But these Jewish women were not alone. Jewish men also responded to the demands of the day fomented by urban growth. In the process, Jews started to change their Judaism, modernizing and Americanizing it. As they turned to other means to assist and educate Jews, synagogues increasingly became sites devoted to religious worship rather than centers of community.

Charleston's moment as the largest Jewish city in North America lasted only a few decades. Its cosmopolitan character that so entranced Jews and to which Jews contributed gradually yielded to a narrow, self-defined Christian society, far less accepting of religious difference or any deviation from the views of the slaveholding elite. Jews stopped coming to Charleston, and some even moved to New York.

After 1820, New York City began to boom as the nation's biggest city and its largest Jewish city. Over the course of a century Jewish immigration would make New York the largest Jewish city in both history and the world. Migration from Europe gradually accelerated in the 1820s and 1830s, picked up momentum in the years before and after the Civil War, and crested in the decades prior to World War I, before ending abruptly in 1924 with legislative restriction. By that time Gotham claimed well over a million Jews. As New York became the unofficial capital of American Jews, Jewish history in the United States acquired a powerful focal point. What happened in New York often reverberated far beyond the Hudson River. Consider another way to imagine the impact of New York City on American Jews: in 1860 "the city sheltered twenty-five percent of the total Jewish population of the United States"; by 1880 that share increased to 33 percent; and by 1920, New York held 45 percent of the total American Jewish population.[27]

Republicanism took different forms among New York Jews compared to those of Charleston and Philadelphia. As Charleston's KKBE was debating reform, New York's first and only congregation, Shearith Israel (Remnant of Israel), was confronting other demands for change. Efforts to integrate different types of Jews soon collapsed in the face of immigration that brought ever-increasing diversity to American cities. It was one thing to compromise on the design of a synagogue interior to accommodate visiting merchants and quite another to make room for growing numbers of poor immigrant Jews who did not speak much English. Although established Jews restructured their congregation, wrote a constitution to guide their governance, and adopted the practice of voting for lay leadership, these democratic impulses could not transcend increasingly sharp class and ethnic distinctions among Jews.[28]

Immigrants from German lands soon outnumbered old-timers with roots in the colonial era. Unfamiliar with American urban practices, they sought solace when gathered in prayer. They asked the leaders of Shearith Israel to be allowed to pray among themselves in a basement room, separate from the rest of the congregation. The congregation's leaders rejected their petition. "Immigration of Ashkenazi Jews created fear," writes historian Howard Rock, "distancing one part of the membership from its republican roots while driving the other into radical republican remedies." Uncomfortable in this established synagogue located a considerable walking distance from their crowded immigrant neighborhood, these German Jews decided to form their own congregation. As newcomers, they yearned for their own place with their own styles of prayer, including less formal worship styles and opportunities to mingle as equals and even to lead should they possess ambition and skills.[29]

So they established Congregation B'nai Yeshurun in 1825. The men not only filed articles of incorporation with the state but also drafted a constitution. Its preamble praised the "wise and republican laws of this country . . . based upon universal toleration given to every citizen and sojourner the right to worship according to the dictate of his conscience." Unlike their brethren in Charleston, the men who established B'nai Yeshurun did not think about the women. Rock characterizes this movement to secede as an example of Jeffersonianism as it took hold among American Jews. Jefferson had affirmed the right to "life, liberty, and the pursuit of happiness." The young men who left Shearith Israel in 1824 over a dispute involving synagogue discipline wanted to abolish class distinctions among Jews. They had absorbed an American ethos of egalitarianism despite their relatively recent arrival in the United States. In their new congregation, all would be equal, and there would be no leadership with special privileges.[30]

By 1827 the congregation had purchased the First Coloured Presbyterian Church on Elm Street in downtown Manhattan. Rather than build a synagogue, B'nai Yeshurun chose to remodel this large church that accommodated six hundred by adding chandeliers and four brick columns. Their decision to repurpose an African American church building marked a Jewish beginning of trading sanctuaries with other urban religious groups. B'nai Yeshurun may have been the first, but it certainly was not the last Jewish congregation to adapt a church into a synagogue, and there would be many synagogues subsequently converted into churches, especially African American ones, in future decades.[31] Yet B'nai Yeshurun's establishment did not promote stability. A year later a number of its restless members left to form another new congregation, Anshe Chesed. Both congregations survived the split and flourished, sustained by increasing numbers of Jewish immigrants in New York City.

The formation of Congregation B'nai Yeshurun initiated fragmentation, experimentation, and multiplication of synagogues in New York and eventually in other cities. As competition among synagogues increased, they championed different religious and civic perspectives. Ideology and theology, religious practices and sacred aesthetics sharpened differences among Jewish congregations and contributed to a burgeoning religious pluralism and experimentation in American cities. Urban Judaism was becoming multiple and malleable.

In the nineteenth century Jewish immigrants sought employment in trade and crafts as they had in the colonial era. Indeed, Jewish participation in commerce extended back centuries to their experience in Europe. But now as they entered trade, many turned to peddling, which took them across an expanding United States. They headed west and south. Since peddlers needed to stock their packs, Jews often participated in creating new towns, such as Talbotton, Georgia, and cities, such as Cleveland and Chicago. Jews figured among the earliest settlers in such cities as St. Louis, San Francisco, and Cincinnati. There they established wholesale and retail businesses, developing networks that connected single young men who were peddling to slightly older Jewish families. In the decade after the Civil War, Jewish enthusiasm for their new urban perspectives, not to mention their newfound prosperity and sense of security, produced a burst of synagogue construction. Jews moved their congregations out of repurposed churches in cities like New York or out of modest rooms above storefronts to build synagogues.[32]

By 1877, Jews lived in a cluster of American cities. New York, of course, led the pack, with approximately 73,000 Jews. But Baltimore, Philadelphia, and Chicago each housed roughly 10,000 Jews, and San Francisco, gateway to the Pacific, was booming with 16,000. (In 1880 the city's population reached 234,000, making San Francisco the ninth largest city in the United States.) Of course, the urbanization of these cities could not yet compare with that in Europe, which had started earlier in the century. European Jews "sought with equal passion the haven of cities that were predominantly Protestant or Catholic, surpassing the attraction to these cities of other ethnic or national minorities." As historian Richard Cohen observes, "The statistics of Jewish urbanization in this period are staggering," with the process accelerating after 1850.[33] Warsaw, the European city with the largest Jewish population, contained 127,000 in 1880, while Vienna and Budapest both had over 70,000 (although New York already was home to more Jews than Berlin). What is equally noteworthy, however, is the dispersed geographic distribution of American Jews: East Coast, West Coast, Midwest, and a borderline southern city. Free to move, Jews repeatedly explored economic opportunities in new cities. This freedom gave Jews choices in constructing both individual and collective spaces.[34]

By 1905, accelerating Jewish migration from abroad produced greater concentration and inaugurated a slightly different, perhaps more familiar geographic picture for the twentieth century. New York now claimed 772,000 Jews, completely dwarfing its closest European rival, Warsaw, with 306,000. Chicago, with 80,000, and Philadelphia, with 75,000, had overtaken San Francisco, previously American Jews' second city, and Baltimore. In their stead emerged Boston (45,000) and St. Louis (40,000). Now roughly half of American Jews lived in just five cities, a trend that would intensify in subsequent decades.[35]

As Jews clustered together, they came to see themselves as a distinctive part of the social fabric of American cities. Their civic enthusiasm for American political values appeared not only in their adoption of constitutions for governing their congregations but also in decisions to locate their synagogues at the city's figurative heart. No longer did they want to blend into the cityscape by drawing on popular Christian architectural models. Now Jews adopted Moorish-style architecture as a way of identifying modern American Judaism as different (Oriental) but also urban. Indeed, Christians accepted it as such, seeing Moorish as the Jewish architectural style.

American Jews' turn to Muslim Spain for architecture articulates a determination by Jews to retain their Jewish identity even as they assimilated into the urban life around them. It reflects as well an idealization of Spanish Jewish culture as both sophisticated and integrated into its surrounding society. But Moorish revival style also draws on Americans' enthusiasm for "Oriental" architecture, perhaps most vividly championed by the impresario P. T. Barnum, who built a three-story villa embellished with bulbous domes, minarets, and arches. New York's Crystal Palace (1854) similarly testified to this vogue. As art historian Olga Bush observes, "These secular buildings were hardly models for imitation in themselves for American Reform Jews." Rather, "the notion of progress associated with both the introduction of 'oriental' style and technological innovations" proved most compelling.[36] The construction of Congregation B'nai Yeshurun's Plum Street Temple in Cincinnati, dubbed an "Alhambra temple with slender pillars and thirteen domes" by its famous rabbi, Isaac Mayer Wise, certainly exemplifies these impulses.[37]

Located on a corner plot facing City Hall across the street from the St. Peter in Chains Cathedral, and standing next to St. Paul Episcopal Church, the Plum Street Temple took its place in 1866 at the city's re-

Corner of Eighth and Plum Streets, Cincinnati. This postcard features the Plum Street Temple on the right, across the street from St. Peter in Chains Cathedral; in the middle of the block is St. Paul Episcopal Church. Courtesy University of Cincinnati.

ligious and civic center. Decades before Americans adopted the concept that Protestantism, Catholicism, and Judaism shared fundamental democratic ideals as part of a "Judeo-Christian Tradition," the Plum Street Temple implemented that notion of three equal religious faiths sustaining American democracy. Standing at the corner of Plum and Eighth Streets and gazing at the four distinctive steeples reaching to the sky (City Hall also had a steeple), a visitor immediately would have recognized each faith through its architectural expression.

Cincinnati architect James Key Wilson designed the lavish synagogue structure in a mix of Moorish Byzantine style, with minarets and elegant arches over its doors. While not the congregation's first synagogue building, it was the one that articulated its rabbi's ambition to lead not only Cincinnati Jews but also American Jews. Isaac Mayer Wise, an immigrant from Germany, arrived in Cincinnati in 1853 after several years in Albany, New York. Wise's reputation as a proponent of religious reforms preceded him. As rabbi of K. K. B'nai Yeshurun, or the Lodge Street Temple as it was then called, Wise devoted himself to revising the character of Jewish religious worship to create what he called a Minhag America, that is, a course of religious prayer and practice representative of American Judaism. Wise prepared a new prayer book, shortened worship services, introduced music, added sermons, and, most radically, brought women down from the balcony to sit next to their male family members. In short, Wise accomplished many of the goals of Charleston's Reformed Society, changes that had also been introduced prior to the Civil War in congregations in New York and other cities. He oversaw construction of the Plum Street Temple, which aimed to demonstrate through its architecture the congregation's national prominence and Cincinnati's increasing importance as a center for American Jews due to Wise's influence.

Nicknamed the Queen of the West, Cincinnati gained a reputation as a center for hog slaughtering. More important for Jews, it stood on rivers separating the slave south (Kentucky) from the free north (Ohio). Cincinnati attracted large numbers of immigrant Germans, both Protestant and Catholic, as well as Irish immigrants. By the late 1880s it grew to a population of almost three hundred thousand, densely packed into the city's hilly terrain. Cincinnati boomed as a center of iron production,

Plum Street Temple interior, looking toward ark and *bima*. Courtesy of the Jacob Rader Marcus Center for the American Jewish Archives, Cincinnati, Ohio.

facilitated by the many railroads that connected the city with other parts of the United States. In those post–Civil War years, its boosters aimed to rival Chicago (population three hundred thousand in 1870). Cincinnati did not outstrip Chicago, but it did become a midwestern hub, a vibrant urban cultural and religious center that claimed prominence nationally, making it attractive as a center for American Judaism.

If Plum Street Temple's exterior reflected Jews' civic engagement and democratic commitment, its interior illustrated emerging Reform Jewish practice. Most of its seats faced the ark, located theater-style behind the raised platform for reading the Torah and for preaching. Pews continued to serve as the financial basis to support a congregation, and seats closer to the ark retained their value as more desirable. But now congregants sat looking forward rather than at each other. Since the reading platform was located at the same end of the synagogue as the ark, there was no need for a procession with the Torah scrolls through the synagogue before reading. As rabbi, Wise assumed visually as much prominence as the Torah scrolls. Their presence behind him amplified his voice and authority.

In this Reform synagogue, Judaism acquired theatrical dimensions. Wise's congregation resembled an audience that listened to sermons and music sung by a choir of men and women rather than participating in noisy prayer. Reform Jews were becoming middle-class American Jews who found religious inspiration through contemporary aesthetics. Worship services increasingly demanded passive attention.

New forms of Jewish spirituality pervaded Plum Street Temple. Music assumed increasing importance, becoming integral to Reform Jewish worship and extending far beyond the chanting of prayers by a *hazzan* or cantor. Plum Street Temple contained an organ and a choir loft where both men and women sang hymns. Women's voices were welcomed in public prayer in this synagogue, not silenced behind the mechitza. The organ's soaring sounds complemented the wonderfully painted ceiling. Candelabras illuminated the brilliant color and elaborate designs of the walls and columns and the ornately carved wooden ark with stained glass tablets of the Ten Commandments above it.

Women's participation in the pews as respectable congregants enhanced Judaism's spirituality in the eyes of Americans. However, women now shared seating with men, but not responsibilities for leadership. In the nineteenth century, Americans increasingly understood Christian spirituality as intimately connected to women.[38] Similarly, Jewish women's presence changed men's behaviors, contributing to greater order and decorum in the synagogue, a goal espoused by many acculturating Jews. Ironically, as historian Karla Goldman observes, "Women gained the right to join men in the shrinking role of congregant," that is, at a point when public prayer as a member of a Jewish community was losing its significance. She goes on to note that bringing women down from the balcony also undermined "the identity of women as a distinct group within the congregation."[39] Joining men in the pews helped weaken Jewish women's consciousness of themselves as set apart, with their own tasks and responsibilities.

Men and women sitting together dispensed with other customs, such as men covering their heads during prayer or wearing a special prayer shawl. Christian visitors to the Plum Street Temple—so distinctive in its external garb—would have felt relatively comfortable once they entered because Jews were adapting its interior sacred forms to conform to tastes familiar to many liturgical Protestants. Yet the temple's grandeur also provided the appropriate site from which to fashion the organizations of American Reform Judaism, beginning with the establishment of the Union of American Hebrew Congregations (UAHC) in 1873, followed two years later by a rabbinical seminary, Hebrew Union College (HUC), in Cincinnati.

Soon a craze for Moorish synagogue buildings took hold among urban Jews. It extended into the early twentieth century and accommodated regional aesthetics as well as different religious perspectives of Jews: Reform, Orthodox, Sephardic, Ashkenazi. In 1860 in New York City, only six of the city's twenty-seven congregations prayed in purpose-built synagogues. Yet in the years immediately following the Civil War, both Catholics and Jews engaged in a building spree. Historians Annie Polland and Daniel Soyer observe that "between 1860 and 1870 synagogue construction, chiefly in New York City, increased New York State's synagogue property value by over 200% to $1,831,950 and doubled its seating capacity from 10,440 to 21,400." Yet these numbers scarcely accounted for the many thousands of immigrant Jews arriving annually, even if one assumes that only men needed to sit in a synagogue. Since many Jewish immigrants continued to pray regularly, they resorted not to congregations and synagogues but to private spaces like prayer rooms for communal worship, often organized around their town of origin. Polland and Soyer argue that Moorish architecture spoke "less to Reform or Orthodox denominational affiliation and more to the freedom and comfort experienced by Jews in the city." These synagogues aimed to create a modern form of New York Judaism that could be transmitted to the next generation.[40]

Nothing worked better to accomplish this goal than neo-Moorish architecture. In adorning their new synagogues with Moorish flourishes, such as lacy finials, horseshoe arches, and interior painting patterns adapted from Spain's Alhambra, Jews made their synagogues immediately distinguishable. No other New York building boasted this style. However, these synagogues did not articulate "an architecture of emancipation," as Scott Lerner argues for European synagogues built in a similar manner.[41] In Europe, Jews were discouraged from using a Gothic style for their synagogues. Adopting a neo-Moorish style announced their urban presence even as it accommodated implicit restrictions on their civic choices. Cohen contends, however, that the enormous Moorish Oranienburgstrasse Synagogue in Berlin radiated a message of "optimism, belief in the process of integration and emancipation, and above all a sense of belonging."[42] In the United States, Jews were free to adopt whatever design pleased them. Hence, while Moorish-style synagogues in American cities shared stylistic elements with a number of grand synagogues built in Europe, these American buildings proclaimed unimpeded democratic sentiments. "If Jews used the Moorish style to proclaim a sense of otherness," argue Polland and Soyer, "it was an otherness that did not threaten their social position." Moorish style synagogues' grand and sumptuous façade signaled Jews' willingness to contribute to their cities and to make them great. Immigration of Jewish architects from Europe to the United States helped to transmit this mode of synagogue building. Henry Fernbach, who came to New York City in 1855, designed several Moorish-style synagogues along with Stern's department store and cast-iron factory buildings.[43]

Moorish architecture appealed as well to successful Jewish immigrants from Eastern Europe who understood it as implicitly Jewish, democratic, modern, and impressive. Following the construction of Reform Temple Emanu-El (1868) and Central Synagogue (1872) in midtown, Eastern European Jews living downtown on New York's Lower East Side decided that they, too, wanted to build a synagogue that paid tribute to both their strong adherence to traditional Judaism and their exuberant embrace of their American identities. So they did. In 1887 they celebrated the dedication of their purpose-built synagogue on Eldridge Street. Here is how Annie Polland, historian of the synagogue, and Daniel Soyer describe the event:

> Arriving on opening day, an uptown reporter from the *American Israelite*, a Reform publication with national circulation, described the architecture as "elegant" and noted the "plentiful supply of air and light from the many and high windows." But he complained that the serene setting failed to inspire decorum among the worshipers, and he sniffed at the women

Central Synagogue on Lexington Avenue and Fifty-Fifth Street in New York City, 1892. Photograph by C. K. Bill. Courtesy Central Synagogue.

> squabbling in the balcony, the babies crying, and the men grasping half-smoked cigars. In retaining Orthodoxy, and the habit of visiting their synagogue daily as opposed to a supposedly more reverential weekly or monthly basis, he suggested, the downtown Jews' Judaism was just as un-American behind an ornate Moorish façade as it was behind the vernacular brick tenement one.[44]

Enthusiasm for Moorish synagogues as expressive of a new urban American Jewish identity cut across religious differences among Jews, highlighting ways that immigration to American cities had disrupted traditional patterns of deference to older, established Jews. A prominent modern Orthodox congregation worshipping in a large and beautiful Moorish synagogue could not be dismissed. Jews were marking the city and were attracting positive attention from Christians, who praised their contribution to the city's spiritual life. The *New York Herald*'s reporter also attended the dedication of the Eldridge Street Synagogue, judging it to be "one of the finest Hebrew places of worship in the city."[45] This represents a far cry from the Touro Synagogue's modesty and simplicity. The reporter's assessment suggests that Orthodoxy and modernity, tradition and prosperity could go hand in hand. In adopting urban innovations introduced initially by Reform Jews, Orthodox Jews indicated their willingness to compete on the city's terrain. Religious changes in Judaism introduced by Reform Jews turned out not to be the only way to reconcile Jewish and American urban identities.

After the Civil War, as synagogues increasingly divided Jews from one another along the lines of ethnicity, theology, and practice, synagogue architecture spoke to both commonalities among Jews and their distinctiveness from Christian Americans. When their fellow urbanites wanted to understand Jews, they usually looked at their religious practices. None stood out so vividly as purpose-built synagogues, especially the neo-Moorish ones. Not only did these buildings make a statement in cities where architecture routinely trumpeted commercial and business success, but they also proclaimed loudly Jewish difference, accomplishment, and persistence in the United States. Substantial synagogues similarly announced the multicultural and religiously plural character of American cities. In some ways worship itself took a backseat to the impressive public spaces visible in these synagogues.

Eldridge Street Synagogue, Lower East Side, New York City.
Photograph by Kate Milford. Courtesy Eldridge Street Project.

While not all congregations opted for Moorish design, synagogues' choice of Moorish architecture addressed common threads uniting Reform and Orthodox Jews. Even though rabbis had started to migrate to the United States in the 1840s, congregational governance remained in the hands of lay leaders, especially those with business acumen acquired in a city's commercial life. Without their accomplishments and generosity, no synagogue building could have been constructed. Yet many of these generous men apparently felt little compunction in moving away from their handsome synagogues. Polland has documented just how quickly some of the leaders behind the construction of the Eldridge Street Synagogue left the Lower East Side for the ample attractions of the new uptown neighborhood of Harlem.[46] Indeed, the willingness of upwardly mobile Jews to leave behind monumental buildings would come to characterize urban Judaism as much as the synagogues themselves.

Congregations did not rely only on men. Increasingly they turned to women to help them navigate the changing contours of religious life. In Reform synagogues women often filled the pews at services. In Orthodox synagogues, even though women lacked a role in public worship, they attended to many activities that kept the congregation running, such as raising funds to support synagogue maintenance.

With so much money and effort invested in building a synagogue, Jews embraced the opportunity to celebrate their achievements. Both when the cornerstone was laid and when the building was complete, elaborately staged performances showcased Jewish aspirations and accomplishments. At these events, Jews invited representatives of the city's political, religious, and cultural life to attend and, on occasion, to speak.

At the dedication ceremony of KKBE's new synagogue building in 1844, Poznanski praised the glories of America, proclaiming, "This synagogue is our temple, this city our Jerusalem, this happy land our Palestine, and as our fathers defended with their lives that temple, that city and that land, so will their sons defend this temple, this city, and this land."[47] Such sentiments gradually spread among Reform Jews. They embraced their cities as fundamentally secure sites where Jewish religious life could flourish, even as their militant language of defense implied some anxiety about attacks. By implication, Poznanski's language suggested that his congregants no longer accepted traditional views of

Jews as a dispersed, exiled people dwelling apart. If the United States was not exile, Jews could be at home in America.

Poznanski also characterized KKBE's synagogue building as a new temple, articulating a locution that would become increasingly commonplace in both the United States and Europe. Associated primarily with Reform Judaism, such terminology that referred to synagogues as "temples" reimagined the meaning of the synagogue as a substitute for the Temple in Jerusalem that had been destroyed by the Romans in 70 CE. Yet gradually other Jews also named their congregations "temples." Sometimes a congregation began to use the term in conjunction with a synagogue's urban location. Hence the Lodge Street Temple in Cincinnati became the Plum Street Temple when the congregation moved to its new building. Although the congregation had a Hebrew name, everyone referred to it by its urban identity.

When Ahawath Chesed (later known as Central Synagogue) in New York City dedicated its synagogue building on Manhattan's Lexington Avenue and Fifty-Fifth Street in 1872, it initiated a process of implementing public ceremonials to forge religious fellowship, holding repeated grand anniversary celebrations in 1922, 1927, 1936, 1946, 1970, and 1979, culminating in 2001 when the congregation celebrated a restored synagogue three years after a devastating fire. Following practices at Plum Street's consecration, the congregation's leaders carried the Torah scrolls into the new building and placed them in the ark. Instead of the traditional seven circuits, reformers reduced them to only three but added other pageantry, such as handing over the keys of the building from the chairman of the building committee to the president of the congregation. At Ahawath Chesed one hundred boys and girls paraded as the cantor chanted Psalm 24, "assisted by a remarkably fine choir and a double orchestra of string instruments."[48] The consecration sermon, in German, uttered in the language these successful Jewish immigrants understood, implicitly affirmed the high value they ascribed to German culture. Reform Jews expressed their religious identity while American urban society promised them democracy. Historian Arthur Goren observes that the sermon praised "America as the promised land of freedom and progress where a Judaism in consonance with the times would flourish."[49]

Interior of Central Synagogue after restoration, looking toward ark and *bima*. Courtesy of Peter Aaron / OTTO.

Goren argues that these ritual performances "wove together the use of Jewish religious objects (the sacred place accorded to the Torah scrolls), biblical metaphor (scriptural passages relating to the temple), a liturgy collated from thanksgiving prayers recited on holidays, and the sermon (an affirmation of an American Judaism)." Jews leaned heavily on American civic ceremonials, like cornerstone-laying ceremonies and a growing fascination of Americans with their anniversaries in the wake of the Civil War. Synagogue dedications articulated Jews' desires to recount their own history in the United States, despite its relative brevity in comparison with the long arc of Jewish history. The presence of public officials followed by detailed, usually favorable accounts in the press highlighted a shared public culture of Jews and Christians where history "served as the medium for proclaiming America's ideals" as well as those of the congregation.[50]

In the years immediately following the Civil War, while New York City had attained a prominence it would not lose as the largest Jewish city in the United States, San Francisco occupied the number two spot, a position it achieved with a much smaller number of Jews. However, the relatively few Jews in San Francisco made up a substantial portion of its population, almost 7 percent. Jews were widely integrated into the city's elites; they handled almost all the region's imports. But Jews also could be found in the city's working classes. San Francisco served as a regional center for the entire Pacific Coast, especially for Jews scattered throughout emerging cities and towns. With western economic and social life focused on San Francisco, Jewish merchant pioneers increasingly invested their profits in manufacturing. Levi Strauss was not alone, though he produced what became the West's "signature apparel."[51] Like New York Jews, San Francisco Jews identified with their city; but unlike New Yorkers, they developed a strong sense of regional identity with the western United States.

As historians have noted, "In contrast to the popular image of the West, the region emerged early in its history as the most urbanized in the country." Jews fit into this "pattern of western development."[52] Jews encountered in San Francisco great ethnic diversity, different from northeastern and midwestern cities. Immigrants from Japan and China, as well as Mexico, formed visible urban cohorts, as did Native Americans and Mexican Americans. Other non-Christian religious groups included Buddhists and Confucians as well as Mormons, in addition to Catholics and many types of Protestants. Jews contributed to this religious and ethnic heterogeneity. By 1905, just before the earthquake, San Francisco supported eight synagogues; its rabbis played active roles confronting the problems of urban life.

An emerging regional consciousness and civic culture shaped Jewish attitudes. Strong feelings of personal freedom, an alliance with other white citizens, an appreciation of the West's physical grandeur, and an orientation toward the Pacific in terms of trade characterized San Francisco's Jews. Perhaps nothing better expressed their profound commitment to California and the West than the stunning stained-glass windows of Sherith Israel. Constructed two years before the earthquake, the synagogue miraculously survived to testify to Jewish enthusiasm for the city and the American West. The stained glass depicts Moses descending with the Ten Commandments to give them to the Israelites. However, he is coming down off the heights not of Mt. Sinai but rather of El Capitan, a famous mountain in Yosemite that was considered impossible to climb. Moses bringing the tablets of the law to California surely expressed an idiosyncratic Jewish attitude to western urbanism.

San Francisco's Temple Emanu-El, like its Reform counterparts in Chicago, New York, Cincinnati, and other cities, encouraged its congregants' wives to emulate their evangelical Protestant, Mormon, and Catholic sisters by organizing public forms of religious ritual. "The second generation of Jewish women, those born in the West, saw themselves not as an insular, stigmatized minority but as the heirs of a mercantile elite," notes historian William Toll. "Assimilation to Western standards of religious pluralism led them to transform their Jewish work from communal benevolence to participation in the wider world of club women." By the end of the century, prosperous Jewish women had created sisterhoods of personal service devoted to helping Jewish immigrants from Eastern Europe. Toll contends that "Jewish social work in the West added an emphasis on religion as a celebratory public ritual," in contrast to Protestant social work that "channeled Christian piety into an ethic of self-control and self-reliance."[53]

But handsome, purpose-built synagogues, so visible and influential

Moses descending El Capitan, Yosemite, stained glass window of Sherith Israel, San Francisco. © Ben Ailes. Courtesy Congregation Sherith Israel.

as monuments to Judaism and its members' success, hardly typified most synagogues in New York or other cities. Instead, most immigrant Jews worshipped in congregations located behind tenement walls, as Polland and Soyer put it. Not all of these congregations actually had synagogues, that is, places consecrated for sacred worship. Many of them were *landsmanshaftn*, organizations of Jews coming from the same Eastern European town or region. By 1910, six hundred congregations existed in immigrant neighborhoods in New York. Most met in rented rooms in tenements or meeting halls, where they served men (*landsleyt*) who shared common immigrant origins.[54] In a sense, these immigrant *landsmanshaft* congregations represented versions of the 1824 request by immigrants to the leaders of Shearith Israel to worship in the basement of the Mill Street Synagogue; only now the intimate space of a basement could be found in a tenement. Within their congregations of fellow immigrants, Jews developed exactly those democratic opportunities for leadership and experienced a type of equality available in urban society the men imagined would be theirs when they established B'nai Yeshurun. "A shortage of qualified clergy," writes Soyer, "allowed ordinary Jewish men to occupy positions of spiritual leadership, especially in smaller congregations." Many Jewish immigrants would use these landsmanshaft congregations as springboards into American culture and as vehicles to help other Jews remaining in their hometowns in Europe.[55]

The impulse to personal service, encouraged by rabbis and enacted by women, built important bridges between Jewish urban communities divided by class and ethnicity. Sponsored by prosperous Reform synagogues, sisterhoods increasingly recruited American-educated Jewish women to direct their attention to their immigrant coreligionists. When the Chicago World's Fair opened in 1893, these articulate middle-class Jewish women seized the occasion to congregate and address social and religious issues of concern. Out of their gathering came the National Council of Jewish Women (NCJW) in 1896. By the early twentieth century the NCJW was sponsoring diverse educational programs for immigrant Jewish women and had stationed a representative at Ellis Island to meet unaccompanied immigrant women to protect them from unscrupulous men who sought to press them into prostitution.[56]

Postcard of Sinai Temple and Social Center, "most liberal congregation in the West," Grand Boulevard and Forty-Sixth Street, Chicago, 1912.

The mood of social action and practical programs that engaged Jewish women in cities across the United States also registered in new forms of synagogue architecture. Jews turned to neoclassical revival styles for their synagogues to announce their urban commitments, just as other Americans did for their civic buildings. Chicago's 1893 exposition, dubbed the White City, inspired public structures of all kinds—town halls, libraries, concert halls, courthouses—to adopt neoclassicism, especially as represented by white buildings with domes, as expressive of the values of American empire.[57]

Temple Sinai in Chicago, led by Rabbi Emil G. Hirsch, enthusiastically embraced this new style with its implied commitment to improve the city. In 1912 the congregation, among the largest in the country, with almost one thousand members, moved into a new building in one of Chicago's "most prestigious neighborhoods." Historian Tobias Brinkmann observes, "The new temple was a status symbol of a congregation strongly committed to Chicago. Architect Alfred S. Alschuler designed a large sanctuary with more than two thousand seats." Even more important, Alschuler restored the Torah scrolls to a place of prominence within the building. They had been removed in a previous effort to transform Sinai into a less Jewish and more universal congregation. Now they returned, although the building's exterior announced its civic, not Jewish, aspirations. "An adjacent building, the Sinai Social Center, accommodated a meeting hall, basketball courts, and a swimming pool." These facilities pointed to a decision to model the new Temple Sinai on the urban institutional church. Hirsch, known as a progressive reformer and renowned speaker, regularly drew to Sinai's standard Sabbath services each Sunday "up to two thousand Christians and unaffiliated Jews," while as many as ten thousand passed "through the state-of-the-art complex" in the 1920s.[58]

Temple Sinai, with its intellectual aspirations, dedication to dialogue with Christians, and commitment to help the working classes, stood outside the Jewish mainstream on the fringes of Reform Judaism. Its distinctive practices, especially its Sunday Sabbath observance, reflect the urban environment from which it grew. In 1861, when Temple Sinai was founded, Chicago was a new industrial city, expanding rapidly, with no established elites and few social barriers—the perfect location for a radical religious experiment. "The congregation reached out to many Chicagoans, supporting in particular civic institutions devoted to education," notes Brinkmann. From its earliest days, "the leaders of a congregation comprising some of the city's wealthiest businessmen spoke up on behalf of the working class."[59] Immigration brought rapid growth to Chicago as the city's population doubled in a decade from 1880 to 1890 and then doubled again by 1900, when it reached two million. Chicago saw some of the most violent social conflicts in American cities in those years, and Hirsch's message of progressive social action, similar to the Protestant social gospel, propelled Sinai to a position of social and political leadership in the city, concerned with educational reform as well as social justice. But by 1910, social anti-Semitism disturbed its congregants and Hirsch sought to energize "Jewish self-respect" among those who listened to his sermons.[60]

Boston's Mishkan Tefila (Tent of Prayer) articulated a comparable vision on a smaller scale, namely that of a Jewish congregation devoted to both Judaism and a new emerging urban neighborhood. Built in 1925 on a hill overlooking the grass and trees of Franklin Park in the middle-class streetcar suburb of Roxbury, Temple Mishkan Tefila's columned

Postcard of Congregation Mishkan Tefila, Elm Hill Avenue, Dorchester, Boston, on the edge of Franklin Park, ca. 1940. Courtesy Dorchester Historical Society.

white façade and graceful steps announced the arrival of Jews as full-fledged citizens of Boston.[61] As literary scholar Barbara Mann notes, "The city increasingly became a stage upon which those more affluent portions of the Jewish community could demonstrate their civic membership."[62] What better stage than a hilltop with a vista of Franklin Park! The congregation's presence at the edge of the park proclaimed that its members at least, if not all Jewish immigrants, no longer were struggling in the old slums of Boston's North and West Ends.

Founded in 1848 by immigrants from Prussia, Temple Mishkan Tefila had moved to Roxbury in 1895, making it one of the earliest congregations to leave the immigrant neighborhood. In its new setting on Elm Hill Avenue, Mishkan Tefila, known as New England's oldest Conservative congregation, sought to position itself as a beacon for diverse Jews moving into the area, which by the late 1930s reached a population of more than seventy thousand. There were as many Jews living in Roxbury-Dorchester in the years prior to World War II as there had been living in New York City after the Civil War. Mishkan Tefila's membership soared to over seven hundred families, especially under the leadership of Rabbi Herman Rubenovitz and his wife, Mignon Rubenovitz.

Both aimed to develop a modern American form of Judaism and shared a common vision of what a Conservative congregation should do. Boston's pervasive anti-Semitism in the interwar years unsettled its Jewish residents. Herman and Mignon Rubenovitz responded to this inhospitable milieu by expanding the synagogue's activities to appeal to Jews across a broad age spectrum. They introduced a successful afternoon Hebrew school for boys and girls and embraced cultural and intellectual endeavors that drew Jews from around Boston who could easily reach the synagogue on public transportation. In 1940, for example, Mignon Rubenovitz established a small museum with prints, ceremonial objects, and illustrated books.[63]

Leading a suburban synagogue located in the city, rabbi and *rebbetzin* (rabbi's wife) worked together to revivify Jewish holidays that were difficult to observe in crowded cities, especially for middle-class Jews uncomfortable performing religious rituals in public. The fall harvest festival of Sukkot, which requires constructing a hut, open to the sky, in which one eats one's meals for a week, had been popular among immigrants, but observance dropped off among their children. "By the 1910s, the tradition of building these booths—these sukkot—was almost forgotten in the middle class Jewish neighborhoods of Upper Roxbury," writes sociologist Gerald Gamm.[64] At that point, the Jewish Men's Club of Mishkan Tefila introduced a congregational *sukkah* (hut) in which members could share a meal and thus fulfill some of the holiday's sacred requirements.[65] According to Mignon Rubenovitz, "To many of the guests, it was the first real Sukkah they had ever seen."[66] This form of collective observance of the holiday would become increasingly widespread, persisting even into the 1970s and 1980s, when a turn to "do-it-yourself" Judaism took hold and inspired Jews living in suburban houses with backyards to build their own sukkah again.

In many ways, the congregation assumed an ambition to be the city's preeminent synagogue, concerned with all elements of urban life. Its public programs and willingness to host meetings of all kinds of groups, both Jewish and nondenominational, exemplified a type of civic Judaism that sought a broad common denominator to unite Jews. Such a version of urban Judaism articulated commitments to the city's politics and to its public schools and support of welfare programs to care for those in need, seeing these as responsibilities of Jews as urban residents to create a genuine society of opportunity. In these aspirations, it was not alone.

In the twentieth century, as Jewish architects accepted commissions to build synagogues, they occasionally even designed sanctuaries for their own congregation. In Detroit, Albert Kahn joined Temple Beth El, the city's oldest congregation, and as a young, aspiring architect, he built its first synagogue at 3424 Woodward Avenue in 1902 in the neoclassical style. It soon proved too small. Under the dynamic leadership of Rabbi Leo Franklin, the Reform congregation expanded rapidly to over eight hundred families. Twenty years later, Beth El moved farther from downtown Detroit out to 8801 Woodward Avenue. Its relocation on the new "piety row" placed it close to some of the more prosperous streetcar suburbs within the city, including the Boston-Edison district where Rabbi Franklin lived. By this time, Kahn had established a national reputation for the automobile factories he had designed for Henry Ford as well as several prominent office buildings in Detroit. He accepted a second commission to design another synagogue building.

This Temple Beth El exemplified a civic spirit analogous to the Plum Street Temple but in a very different architectural language. With a rabbi deeply involved in Detroit's politics, on speaking terms even with the notorious anti-Semite Henry Ford, Temple Beth El announced a Jewish vision of urban life that celebrated the city's manifold opportunities for social mobility. Kahn's 1921 building resembled a federal building or massive post office, much like Temple Sinai. Nothing marked it as distinctively Jewish other than "Temple Beth El" carved on its lintel. For instance, neither Stars of David nor quotes from the Bible ornamented the synagogue exterior. Its eight massive stone columns shielding a portico and its broad rows of stairs leading up to three huge wooden double doors expressed a deep commitment to urban life. A visitor walking the sidewalk in front of Temple Beth El might have been inspired to climb these impressive steps to view the city from its elevation. But Temple Beth El did not stand alone on Woodward. Across the street the Jewish Community Center offered recreational facilities, classes for immigrants, and diverse charitable activities designed to help those in need. In 1925, Rabbi Franklin initiated regular broadcasts of worship services over the radio, reaching out to listeners in their homes. Like Mishkan

Tefila, this twentieth-century synagogue announced its civic intentions, its understanding of modern American Judaism as committed to the public welfare. Urbanism and Judaism intertwined.

Inside the main sanctuary figurative paintings decorated the four corners of the ceiling beneath a huge dome. The choice of figures, like an organ, expressed Reform Jews' rejection of aniconic traditions of synagogue decoration. Unlike Moses descending from El Capitan, however, Temple Beth El's imagery focused not on western lands but on biblical motifs and, significantly, on immigration, placing this formative exodus from Europe in dialogue with the biblical Exodus from Egypt. This vast social movement that brought almost two million Jews to the United States was under siege from restrictionists and anti-immigrant proponents—Americans who did not like Jews and other foreigners—even as Beth El commissioned a painting of a young immigrant man, implicitly Jewish, as signified by his cap and fingers intertwined with a book, gazing longingly at the Statue of Liberty from a ship. The integration of immigration into the sacred consciousness of American Jews at the moment when it was attacked, and by Jews who often belonged to a second or third generation born in the United States, articulated a new dimension to American Judaism. Beth-El's painting envisioned immigration as providential and recast the new promised land as a nation of immigrants, foreigners from other shores. It expanded Poznanski's vision of "this happy land" by explicitly welcoming these strangers, reminding congregants to make common cause with those who sought a haven on American soil.[67]

If Detroit, the Motor City, represented one type of Reform Jewish engagement with a city defined by a single industry, Los Angeles exemplified a very different type of urban regionalism. What the automobile industry was to Detroit, the movie industry was to Los Angeles. But unlike in Detroit, where relatively few Jews found work with the large automobile factories but instead earned a livelihood from other, often related, occupations, in Los Angeles Jews played key roles in the motion picture industry, holding jobs in all aspects of the business, even the very top ones as producers and heads of major studios. As Hollywood expanded in the 1920s, Jews organized a number of congregations. But the first

Temple Beth El interior, painting of Jewish immigrant arriving at Ellis Island. Author photo.

one to attract the support of wealthy movie producers, the Wilshire Boulevard Temple, also best exemplifies the impact of popular urban culture on American Judaism.

As with the Plum Street Temple and Temple Sinai, the Wilshire Boulevard Temple, completed in 1929, stood as a monument to its ambitious rabbi, Edgar Magnin. He had grown up in San Francisco and arrived in 1915 as assistant rabbi of Congregation B'nai B'rith (Sons of the Covenant), the earliest synagogue established in Los Angeles, dating back to the nineteenth century. Magnin dreamed of a new temple building that would connect older Jewish families in Los Angeles with Hollywood newcomers. The Wilshire Boulevard Temple brokered that relationship by enlisting the son of the congregation's first rabbi as architect and the financial support of movie industry men, especially the Warner brothers and their wives. Magnin used his pulpit to broadcast a national message of a popular contemporary Judaism, one congruent with the narrative biblical murals by Hugo Ballin that adorned the massive sanctuary. Magnin hoped that the murals of biblical figures that look as if they came out of central casting (or at least a Cecil B. DeMille epic) would stimulate "the imagination and a curiosity for deeper knowledge about our own traditions." As he noted, this was "an age in which people desire visualizations," so the synagogue should "bring a better message to its people by falling in line with this trend."[68]

Borrowing techniques from the motion pictures and movie palaces, the Wilshire Boulevard Temple promoted an emotionally expressive Judaism. Eschewing intellectualism, its aesthetic favored drama and elegance. The temple featured an eclectic mixture of styles—Byzantine, Romanesque, art deco, and southwestern, with stucco exterior walls. It towered over the modest urban landscape of what was then western Los Angeles. Inside, a massive one-hundred-foot dome created an awe-inspiring space with black marble columns, teak doors, gold fixtures for the ark, and bronze chandeliers. A visitor could only marvel at its spectacular beauty. Although Technicolor and wide screens had yet to be invented in 1929 when the temple was dedicated, its exuberance was designed to take one's breath away. If this was Judaism, it offered another world, quite apart from the ordinary one of Los Angeles, a world closer to the imagination and mystery of the movies. When Jews go to a

Wilshire Boulevard Temple, Los Angeles. Located beyond the streetcar line, it presaged the city's future dependence on automobiles. Courtesy Wilshire Boulevard Temple.

synagogue service, Magnin explained, "they must come out touched. If they don't come out laughing or crying, then there's something wrong." Magnin wanted his congregants to leave services with "some feeling of 'I'm glad I'm a Jew. There *is* something to life, some meaning.'"[69]

By the 1920s Jews started to look to their urban synagogues to fulfill additional roles in their lives. They wanted a synagogue to be a place not only to pray but also to play, a place for study and socializing, a space that allowed sacred and secular to coexist and comingle. The idea of a synagogue center resembled Sinai's institutional congregation, except that it focused particularly on neighborhood Jews. Articulated most influentially by Rabbi Mordecai M. Kaplan when he worked to plan the Jewish Center on Eighty-Sixth Street in Manhattan, the synagogue center concept imagined that local Jews would spend many hours at their synagogue. Family memberships would express a new reality that both women and children were welcome in the synagogue.

Kaplan's vision soon became known as the *shul* (synagogue) with a pool and school. His vision, compatible with modern Orthodoxy, articulated a contemporary approach to Judaism as a way of life. In the synagogue center Jews might re-create something evoking the total world that had been Judaism as a religious civilization. Modern Orthodox Jews accepted their city's heterogeneity, claiming that they could live fully observant Jewish lives without sacrificing urbanity's pleasures and rewards.[70] Yet they also evinced a willingness to experiment. Their support transformed Kaplan's ideal into a multistory Jewish Center, dedicated in 1918. But scarcely had they settled into this unusual synagogue building than Kaplan quarreled with the lay leadership and left to form the Society for the Advancement of Judaism a few blocks away.[71]

As the nation's largest city, New York encouraged diversity and experimentation. The city's cultural prominence derived in part from its size and its commercial, financial, and industrial might. After World War I, New York City's Jewish population skyrocketed as Jews came to form over 25 percent of the city's population. Even after drastic restrictions on immigration in 1924, their numbers continued to climb since roughly 70 percent of new arrivals decided to stay in the city.

Numbers alone do not tell the whole story, though it is impossible to ignore such a concentration of Jews. More Jews lived in New York than in any European city. Neither Warsaw nor Paris, neither Vienna nor Budapest, neither Berlin nor Odessa—none could approach New York. In fact, more Jews lived in New York by 1920 than lived in England or France, Germany or Austria, Hungary or Italy. Their population was approaching two million by 1940, when more American Jews lived in New York—around 40 percent of them—than anywhere else in the United States. If American Jews had a capital city, it was New York.[72]

New York City consisted of five boroughs, but in those years the ones that mattered to Jews were Manhattan, the Bronx, and Brooklyn. In fact, the synagogue that perhaps embodied the concept of Kaplan's synagogue center most fully was constructed on Eastern Parkway in Brooklyn in 1921 in the Jewish neighborhood of Crown Heights, miles away from Manhattan's Jewish Center.

Its history began a month after the armistice ending World War I was signed, when thirteen men gathered at the home of Louis Cohen on President Street to discuss the prospects of establishing a Jewish center for their up-and-coming neighborhood. Samuel Rottenberg, an ardent advocate of the center ideal, explained its attractions to the gathering. The center was to be more than a synagogue, because all of the men were members of a synagogue. These friends came to the meeting because they wanted to create a new Jewish organization that would address their needs as successful businessmen, family men, committed Jews, and patriotic Americans. They self-consciously chose to stake out a fresh path in what they imagined as a suburban milieu, albeit a suburb located on subway lines only a half hour from Lower Manhattan. Crown Heights was different from its residential neighbor, densely populated immigrant Brownsville; still filled with empty sites and even the occasional farm, Crown Heights appeared to be a lush and potentially prosperous urban wilderness. As I've written elsewhere, "Confident of their future success, they decided to create a model Jewish center and to limit membership to those able to afford not less than a $500 membership fee and initial minimum dues of $100 per member, not inconsiderable sums. Each man pledged to bring twenty-five potential members to a meeting the following week."[73]

The next week, with a much larger group, discussion grew heated. Cohen wanted to follow the model of the modern Orthodox Jewish Center in Manhattan and to limit membership to those living within walking distance. He assumed that members would observe traditional restrictions on travel on the Sabbath. Others wanted to set the limit to membership at two hundred, which meant doubling the radius around the center from five blocks to ten. This debate over membership spoke to the heart of synagogue organization and positioned the synagogue in a new relationship to urban space. Cohen's ideal center was intimate and accessible, a place where children starting at the age of four would be cared for while their parents engaged in activities, social, religious, or recreational, day or night. A Jewish center had to exude *yidishkeyt* (Jewishness) as a home away from home, but it also had to embody American upper-middle-class notions of comfort and status. The more expansive vision imagined the synagogue center as a magnet for Jews scattered far less densely, who would come to make the synagogue their singular Jewish address.

However, the issue that stirred the most debate revolved less around the complete ideal of Jewish center—after all, it was hard to argue with Rottenberg's prescription that it "be everything a man needs in the way of recreation, physical and mental, . . . from his infancy to old age"—than around financing. How was membership to be understood? Did one buy a seat like on the stock exchange, where everyone was equal, and one could then sell the seat when one left, or were some seats better than others and one merely rented the seats, which remained the property of the center? In the end, hierarchy won over democracy since those who were willing to pay more wanted to get better seats, that is, seats in the front of the sanctuary near the Holy Ark. In this bidding, Rottenberg trumped Cohen, pledging a $2,500 contribution versus Cohen's $1,500.

The Brooklyn Jewish Center integrated physical culture (it had a swimming pool in the basement along with a gym) with religious culture (the sanctuary on the second floor), education (a progressive parochial school called the Center Academy as well as an afternoon Hebrew school and Institute for Adult Jewish Studies), and opportunities for socializing (a kosher restaurant within the synagogue). Its new approach accompanied innovations in religious services, such as Friday evening services featuring music, a lecture, abbreviated prayer, and socializing with food. Unlike Reform congregations, however, the Brooklyn Jewish

Brooklyn Jewish Center pool; photo taken during hours reserved for men.
P297. Courtesy the Library of the Jewish Theological Seminary.

Center did not acquire an organ. Instead it followed updated modern Orthodox practice in which a cantor sang traditional and modern melodies, chanted the prayers, and conducted a male choir.

The men and women who built the Brooklyn Jewish Center possessed a sense of the boldness of their vision. They were willing to invest in such an experimental synagogue center because it spoke to their identities as American Jews and New Yorkers. Surrounded by comfortable single-family homes and upper-middle-class apartment buildings, the Brooklyn Jewish Center dominated its stretch of Eastern Parkway, a broad, tree-lined avenue ideal for Sabbath and holiday strolls. The center offered every amenity one might desire. It was more than a settlement house or community center or public library or public school. As a neighborhood Jewish hub, the center welcomed all types of Jews, especially to its popular Monday night forums that featured prominent intellectuals, many of them not Jewish.

This new type of synagogue drew on Kaplan's prototype as well as examples of Christian practices visible in the city. Protestants had developed the "institutional church" to reach out to residents with a range of social services, often helping people to cope with the hardships of urban life. The synagogue center adapted this multiservice and multipurpose idea. Its manifold activities required an extensive professional staff, not just a rabbi and cantor, but also a physical education director (a position that evolved into executive director in charge of social and recreational activities), a manager for the dining room and *mashgiach* (supervisor of *kashrut*) for the kitchen, a janitor, and office staff.

Although neighborhood residents were invited to participate in classes, hold their organizational meetings in the center's rooms, and attend late Friday night services or Monday evening lectures by a prominent personality, the Brooklyn Jewish Center catered to its members. At least a quarter of these one thousand members in 1925 were successful manufacturers, and another sizable percentage were professionals, lawyers and doctors. Together with merchants, realtors, and building contractors, these occupational categories accounted for over half of the membership. Although prosperous and secure in the upper reaches of the middle class, many had completed only grade school.[74] Yet they aspired to upper-class culture and eagerly attended opera and symphony concerts, the theater and art museums, cynosures of urban elite culture.

They were equally devoted to Judaism. Their support and participation sustained the Brooklyn Jewish Center. They sent their children to its Hebrew school and to the Center Academy, a progressive Jewish elementary school; they attended Sabbath and holiday services in the elegant sanctuary; they thrilled to the musical voice of cantor Rubin Tucker (Richard Tucker when he left the congregation for a career at the Metropolitan Opera); and they enjoyed theatrical productions of the Center Players led by Moss Hart (before he departed to produce shows on Broadway). Most of all, they treasured their rabbi, Israel Levinthal, a second-generation Jew and son of a rabbi who grew up in Philadelphia and understood the challenges they faced living as Jewish New Yorkers.

The synagogue center articulated a new urban religious ideal, embraced by many second-generation Jews in the years after World War I. It would become the dominant model of the synagogue in the post–World War II years, transported by a new generation out to the suburbs. Pioneered in urban streetcar suburbs in such neighborhoods as Crown Heights and Flatbush in Brooklyn, synagogue centers responded to competition from city commercial recreation by incorporating entertainment under their Jewish auspices. Theater, higher education, lectures, dances, and music, not to mention sports and the pleasures of eating out in a kosher restaurant, all could be consumed and enjoyed as part of a single, albeit expensive, membership. The rise of the synagogue center measures the growing prosperity of American Jews, especially the children of immigrants. They transformed the synagogue into a family-based institution.

In an era of women's suffrage, synagogue centers incorporated women into their leadership as wives and especially as mothers. The Brooklyn Jewish Center introduced consecration services for girls even as it retained gender separation. As it modified tradition, the center steered a middle path of compromise guided by Rabbi Levinthal. Its pluralist seating in the sanctuary accommodated those men and women who wanted to sit as a family unit (in the center) and those men and women who preferred to pray separately (on either side of the center seating, men on the left, women on the right). Similarly, the pool provided hours restricted just for women and other hours reserved for men. Yet the impetus of the synagogue center, as articulated in the writing of Mordecai Kaplan and embodied in the Brooklyn Jewish Center, urged Jews to live Judaism wholeheartedly, to play as Jews as well as pray as Jews and to do so in an American urban style.

As Plum Street Temple proclaimed a new type of American Judaism that became institutionalized as Reform in the latter half of the nineteenth century, so did the Brooklyn Jewish Center express a form of American Judaism for the twentieth century initially considered modern Orthodox but subsequently known as Conservative. In both cases, innovative urban synagogues provided models. As Reform became identified with Cincinnati through its institutions and especially its rabbinical seminary, so did Conservative Judaism become identified with New York City through the Synagogue Council of America (an organization of Conservative synagogues) and especially the Jewish Theological Seminary of America, which trained Conservative rabbis. As Reform temples spread throughout the country, so did Conservative synagogue centers. As Reform temples and their rabbis participated in the civic life of American cities, supporting progressive efforts to improve urban life and aid the poor, so did Conservative synagogue centers and their liberal rabbis encourage Zionist endeavors to establish a homeland in the land of Israel. The new urban synagogue center, despite the cost it took to build, became a prototype for a modern American Judaism that would prove apt when Jews and Judaism moved to the suburbs.

New York City also incubated alternative models to the synagogue center, new forms of spiritual or ethnic community extending beyond the congregation. After he left the Jewish Center, Kaplan decided to found a new religious movement, the Society for the Advancement of Judaism (SAJ), that would unite different segments of American Jews. He wanted to reconstruct Judaism, but he did not think that he could do it through the synagogue. So he looked to the religious movement spawned by Reform Judaism in New York City in the nineteenth century for a kind of prototype: the Ethical Culture movement founded by Felix Adler.

Adler rejected God and Reform Judaism's emphasis on Jews as the chosen people in favor of a universalist ethics. He built a school and lecture hall across Central Park from Temple Emanu-El, where his father had served as rabbi.[75] For Adler, who also taught philosophy at the university level, propagation of ethical ideas through education and lecturing took precedence over prayer or worship. While Kaplan admired Adler's boldness, he rejected his theology. Kaplan believed firmly that Judaism could be revised to speak to an emerging generation of native-born American Jews. He aimed to institutionalize pluralism and diversity by designing a kind of Jewish theological umbrella to unite Jews. So he decided to build a modest synagogue as a laboratory where he could preach and experiment with new liturgies (including introducing the first bat mitzvah), classrooms where he could teach, offices where he could edit a biweekly magazine, *The Reconstructionist*, and a social hall for celebrations.

In 1934 Kaplan published *Judaism as a Civilization: Toward a Reconstruction of American Jewish Life*. In it he argued that Jews in the United States of necessity lived in both American and Jewish civilizations. If Judaism was an evolving religious civilization, then it embraced all aspects of life: social, political, cultural, and, of course, religious. Living in two civilizations characterized U.S. Jews; Jews living in the *yishuv* (settlement) in

Detail of kibbutz harvest from *Elements of Palestine: Old and New*, mural by Temima Gezari in the Society for the Advancement of Judaism, New York City. Courtesy *The Reconstructionist*.

Palestine had returned to living in one civilization—a new Zionist Jewish civilization where Hebrew was the spoken language of everyday life and not just the language of prayer and study.

Kaplan also argued for the importance of art and aesthetics in contemporary Judaism. He commissioned a synagogue mural by the artist Temima Nimtzowitz (Gezari) titled *Elements of Palestine, Old and New*. He aimed to beautify the SAJ sanctuary, not with stained glass reflecting Christian culture or Hollywood versions of biblical epics but with paintings inspired by a new Zionist Jewish culture growing in Palestine. In fact, Nimtzowitz had been stimulated as much by her experience working with radical Mexican muralist Diego Rivera as she had been by her eight months spent painting in the land of Israel. Her imagery contrasted Jewish Old World types—elderly men studying Talmud, for example—with Jewish scientific, technical, and academic achievements. The large center panel portrayed Jewish men and women on a kibbutz (a collective farm) harvesting the land's abundant produce.[76]

These diverse versions of urban Judaism traveled to new regions after World War II as thousands of Jews left their homes in the large, crowded cities of the Northeast and Midwest for tantalizing sun-splashed cities that they had discovered during their military service. Both Miami Beach, where the Army Air Corps trained its officers and billeted them in the resort hotels, and Los Angeles, which thousands viewed from troop trains and depots en route to the Pacific theater, attracted Jewish migrants.

They joined many thousands streaming to these cities to craft new lives for themselves and their families after military service. Soon Jews started to build synagogues in Miami and Los Angeles that reflected their new perspectives: willingness to experiment, eclecticism, and eagerness to follow charismatic rabbis with visions of a multifaceted Judaism for the postwar world.

Rabbi Leon Kronish came down to Miami Beach even before the war had ended. He started in the summer of 1944 at Beth Sholom Center (House of Peace), whose name reflected more of its ambitions than realities. Located on Forty-First Street in a non-Jewish section of Miami Beach, the small congregation seemed to defy possibilities. At that time few Jews lived in the city, which had a reputation as both anti-Semitic and antiblack. Kronish was ready for the challenge.

Kronish sought to create a liberal congregation with a strong Zionist commitment affiliated with the Reform movement in the image of his mentor, Rabbi Stephen S. Wise. So he urged the members to change the name to Temple Beth Sholom. But his congregants thought the idea of a liberal Jewish congregation did not match the ideology of a Reform Jewish congregation. To their mind, the latter evoked elitism, a religious service devoid of Hebrew, non-Zionism, strict rules of decorum, and a formal quality of worship. It took several years before Kronish convinced them to choose Reform, and as soon as they did, he pointedly referred to Temple Beth Sholom as liberal.

Liberal Judaism in Miami Beach in the 1950s and 1960s meant an open, democratic synagogue, one that welcomed and educated girls on an equal plane with boys. Temple Beth Sholom's lively, low-slung domed synagogue contained a series of parabolic arches filled with multicolored glass in hexagonal interlocked Stars of David. The sanctuary adopted the popular theater format with all seats facing front. In addition the synagogue incorporated a social hall designed to expand the space for worship. Percival Goodman, a Jewish architect who designed the building, produced a futuristic space, playful and appropriate for Miami Beach leisure culture.[77]

Leon Kronish and his wife Lillian filled that space with experimentation: a cantata for the holiday of Shavuot (Weeks), celebrating when Jews received the Torah from God at Mount Sinai, a new *megillah* (scroll) in-

Temple Beth Sholom interior, Miami Beach, Florida.
© Paul Rocheleau. Courtesy Paul Rocheleau.

terpreting the holiday of Purim, a special bat mitzvah class and program, women at the pulpit during the High Holidays. At the same time, both rabbi and rebbetzin encouraged congregants to observe Jewish holidays at home, guiding them in how to conduct a Passover *seder*, for example. In short, Temple Beth Sholom promoted the art of Jewish living, an aesthetic experience simultaneously joyous, spiritual, and homey. The synagogue also did its best to lower all barriers to participation, interpreting a populist ethos to mean no financial burdens, no tuition fees for school, no assigned pews. So, too, did rabbi and rebbetzin invite newcomers to Miami Beach to make their American society more equitable.[78]

One of their most important efforts involved a court case against Christian religious practices in the public schools. The defendants included two congregants, Philip and Thalia Stern. Thalia played a leading role in antinuclear activism in Miami together with other women, both Jewish and Christian. She also worked with African Americans to promote integration through the Congress on Racial Equality. Championing separation of church and state reflected her liberal Jewish commitments, as well as those of Temple Beth Sholom.[79] The case, *Chamberlin v. Dade County*, challenged outspoken expressions of Christian piety in the schools, including religious services conducted over a loud speaker, nativity plays at Christmas, pressure to attend school during the High Holidays, religious symbols in classrooms. In fact, Christian values permeated Miami's public school day, which began with Bible reading, often accompanied by prayer, and for older children included short sermonettes. Then came the Lord's Prayer in its Protestant iteration. At Christmas and Easter schoolwide assemblies celebrated the holidays with music and drama.[80]

Kronish spoke as a witness in the trial and tried to convince the national rabbinical associations to urge local rabbis to support separation of church and state. Although the case reached the Supreme Court, it arrived too late to be of historic significance. Decisions in two earlier cases banned Bible reading and the Lord's Prayer in public schools, and the Court refused to address some additional issues raised by *Chamberlin*, such as display of religious symbols, baccalaureate services, singing of religious hymns, instruction in the dogma of the nativity and resurrection, as well as religious tests for teachers and religious censuses of students.

Urban Judaism in the postwar era became identified with separation of church and state, a position that emerged out of a profound Jewish commitment to both public education and liberal religious values nurtured in America's cities. This widespread Jewish position articulated, in twentieth-century language, sentiments similar to those of the Newport congregation in 1790. Responding to challenges of city living, Jews held understandings of freedom of religion that continued to evolve. Yet they retained their goals of integrating into the United States and securing Jewish life.[81]

That security could not be assumed. Even as Jews mounted challenges to reigning Christian public practices in the schools, they faced attacks on their synagogues by anti-Semitic white supremacists, who condemned Jews as supporters of African American equality. Ten percent of the bombs between 1954 and 1959 took aim at urban Jewish targets, including several Miami synagogues. However, the bombing of the Temple in

Atlanta attracted the most attention because of its location at the heart of the civil rights struggle.

With its columned façade and Romanesque architecture, the Temple committed itself to the city of Atlanta, "the city too busy to hate," as its leaders like to say. But this identification with the city's white majority and its culture could not be sustained in the 1950s as African Americans pushed ever more forcefully for integration. "The upwardly mobile Jewish families of the Temple—with reason to fear for their own security—placed their delicate social status and physical safety at risk by timorously, even unhappily, taking the side of the African Americans in what was then known as the 'Negro question,'" writes Melissa Fay Greene.[82]

Both Atlanta and the Temple tried to ignore racial questions, but Rabbi Jacob Rothschild would not let them. As Greene writes, "Rothschild understood the black citizens to be the wronged, the oppressed, the downtrodden spoken of by the Jewish prophets. And he heard the exhortations to help them." In moving from anxiety and reluctance to take on crucial issues of the day toward engagement with the civil rights struggle, congregants followed the same path as other Atlantans. Ironically, "Temple Jews understood that their jumping onto Rothschild's racial justice bandwagon would render them—in the eyes of white Christian Atlanta—more alien, more suspect, more *Jewish* than if the men were to grow beards and sidelocks and the women to don kerchiefs, all of them trudging downtown to sell pickles and used pots from pushcarts."[83]

The bombing of the Temple on October 12, 1958, provoked outrage and sympathy, energizing Christians throughout the city to change their behaviors (although a jury of twelve white men acquitted the defendant after a brief half-hour discussion). Atlantans saw the dark side of their resistance to integration. As a result of the bomb, the Temple emerged as an institution leading the city toward a more righteous stance. Rothschild repeatedly spoke out in his sermons in favor of integration, nudging congregants to take a stand in favor of equality. In 1960 he and his wife Janice befriended Martin Luther King, Jr. and his wife Coretta Scott King, inviting them home to dinner. Gradually, the Temple fulfilled the promise of its neoclassical architecture: it was indeed a crucial civic institution in Atlanta that helped to alter the course of the city's history.[84]

Los Angeles brought different challenges, perhaps best exemplified by another rabbi who admired Stephen S. Wise. Rabbi Isaiah Zeldin, a product of an Orthodox New York City home and training at Hebrew Union College as a Reform rabbi, arrived in Los Angeles in 1953. Energetic and entrepreneurial, he promoted the growth of Reform Judaism in the city. He wanted Reform Jews to compete with Conservative Jews by training rabbis, helping to convince Jack Skirball, a rabbi turned movie producer, to transform the fledgling College of Jewish Studies into the California School, a branch of HUC.

Zeldin came away from this experience convinced that education had to become a central pillar for Judaism in postwar America. In his mid-forties, he set out to build his own congregation named in honor of Rabbi Stephen S. Wise based on this conviction. Zeldin developed a wide variety of educational offerings for all ages, from infants and toddlers to grandparents. "We take you from the sperm to the worm," joked a temple official. Zeldin kept on expanding the types of educational programming available, including summer camps, holiday workshops, special programs for teenagers, a parenting center for infants and mothers, a Daddy and Me program for toddlers and fathers, and a group for widowers with small children. Within five years of its founding in 1964, the Stephen S. Wise Temple schools enrolled 4 percent of all Jewish children in Los Angeles religious schools, drew 250 regularly to adult education classes, and sent a cohort of teenagers from its Hebrew high school to Israel each year.[85]

"Our goal here is to help them feel as comfortable about their Jewishness as they do about being Americans," Zeldin explained, echoing Kaplan's concept of living in two civilizations. "Judaism becomes an integrated way of life rather than a compartmentalized life experience relegated to Friday night services." Adopting a policy that opened programs to nonmembers, the Wise Temple reaped substantial rewards in expanding membership. By the mid-1970s, the temple had over twelve hundred members; ten years later membership hovered around ten thousand.[86]

The Stephen S. Wise Temple recast much of what the Brooklyn Jewish Center developed, but instead of creating a synagogue center that encouraged Jews to discover American pleasures such as recreation or dining out or stimulating lectures or high culture, it reversed the process.

Zeldin produced a synagogue center that encouraged American Jews to encounter the rewards of being Jewish. To do so, he placed education, rather than worship, at the heart of the synagogue. He even established an all-day school, roughly parallel to the Center Academy. Then in 1990 Wise Temple founded a high school.

Zeldin recognized that without education, American Jews no longer would understand what it meant to be Jewish, or even how to be Jewish. They certainly would not be comfortable being Jewish. Yet he grasped as well that American Jews were now engaged in a search for personal meaning like other Americans. In a city like Los Angeles—diverse, dispersed, heterogeneous, containing ambitious newcomers without roots—Judaism needed to take form in a reimagined synagogue. The old styles would not do. So the Wise Temple adapted the concept of a college campus, building not a single, multiuse synagogue, but rather a series of interconnected buildings on a mountain overlooking the 405 freeway, midway between the San Fernando Valley and the city's western neighborhoods. The campus framework drew on Jews' increasingly common experience of attending college, strengthened the temple's educational focus, and provided opportunities for intimate encounters for spiritual seekers. It also reflected the new urbanism of Los Angeles.

Los Angeles combined the attractions of suburbanization, including private home ownership and an infrastructure built around the automobile, within an urban milieu; but older cities, especially those in the Midwest such as Cleveland, Detroit, St. Louis, Cincinnati, and even Chicago, gradually lost population to their suburbs. Jews left many American cities in the postwar years; often they took their synagogues with them. Although these synagogues usually incorporated some distinctive elements forged in the urban environment, they stood in a vastly different milieu of private homes. Most Jews no longer walked to synagogue; they drove. Huge parking lots accommodated congregants' cars. And without the streets to sustain them, synagogue architecture increasingly evoked different forms of spirituality, even paying attention to nature's power to inspire.

When Jews moved to the suburbs, they left behind cities struggling with financial troubles, declining populations, increasing numbers of African Americans and Hispanic immigrants, as well as industrial and commercial abandonment. Often they sold their synagogues to Christian churches, recapitulating the nineteenth-century process of repurposing religious buildings.[87]

But the postwar years also brought Jewish newcomers to American cities. Prior to 1965 and the liberalization of immigration laws, the most visible new arrivals were Hasidic Jews. They settled in poor immigrant neighborhoods, such as Williamsburg in Brooklyn, but they also found a niche in middle-class areas in Brooklyn, such as Borough Park. By 1980 over seventy thousand Jews lived in that neighborhood supporting around 150 congregations. "The names of the latter read like a travelogue through the *shtetlach* [towns] of prewar eastern Europe: Amshinov, Belz, Bobov, Bratzlov, Chust, Debrecen, Ger, Keresztur, Lubavitch, Munkacs, Nyitra, Pap, Rodomsk, Skvir, Szatmar, Temeshvar, Ungvar, Viznitz," observed sociologist Egon Mayer.[88] New York City streets so compressed Europe's geography that different sects that previously had lived hundreds of miles apart now shared the same sidewalks. The presence of so many Hasidic survivors of the Holocaust gradually transformed neighborhoods into versions of an urban shtetl (small town). In Brooklyn could be found dozens of small, intimate *shtibls* (prayer rooms), usually located in private homes or above shops.[89]

In the 1950s, Menachem Mendel Schneerson ascended to the leadership of the Lubavitch Hasidim as their Rebbe and gradually introduced American urban religious innovations. Some seemed to resemble Salvation Army techniques, converting the city's streets into potentially sacred cathedrals of the open air in efforts to reach sinners.[90] Schneerson was not interested in gentile sinners, though he considered the world corrupt; rather he wanted to find irreligious Jews and ignite their Jewish souls. But he was not going to wait for them to come to synagogue; instead, he would send his distinctively clad emissaries—as recognizable as any Salvation Army lad or lass—out onto the city's streets. Inspired by President John F. Kennedy's proposal for a Peace Corps, the Rebbe's mitzvah campaign broadcast a message of redemption to urban Jews.[91]

By the 1970s Lubavitch young men could be seen in Manhattan standing on crowded sidewalks outside of Mitzvah Mobiles. These step vans held prayer books and prayer shawls, *tefillin* (the two small boxes containing quotations from scripture and bound with leather straps on the arm and forehead) and Sabbath candles, as well as inspirational literature. Large enough to accommodate men standing, the vehicles doubled as private prayer rooms on wheels, an impressive modification of America's booming car culture. "Excuse me, sir, are you Jewish?" the young Lubavitch men would ask a passerby. If the answer were affirmative, they would inquire if the man that morning had put on tefillin as required when saying morning prayers. When the answer was negative, they would urge their interlocutor to step into the van and lay tefillin, promising to help demonstrate how to wind the leather straps and say the appropriate prayers. The Mitzvah Mobiles were designed to reach unaffiliated and unobservant American Jews to bring them back to Judaism. "Schneerson wanted an alternative army to the Zionist one," argue sociologists Samuel Heilman and Menachem Friedman, "one that did not move by firepower but was driven by spiritual power, one that he commanded and which brought not destruction before victory but mitzvahs before redemption."[92] Schneerson's vision inspired his Hasidim, who recruited hundreds and gradually thousands, drawing both men and women back to a pietist, strictly observant form of Judaism.

Yet this campaign of service to Jews everywhere located its headquarters in a relatively nondescript building that served as home, office, and synagogue. As Hasidim adjusted to urban America in the postwar decades, they rehabilitated and enlarged the shtibl as a model for prayer and community. Small, intimate, informal, and male, the shtibl represented the polar opposite of the synagogue center. It was literally a home, a return to European forms, using private personal space as a synagogue. Although Hasidim were visible on the streets of the city, the men identified by their black suits, white shirts, full beards, and hats, they did not base their Judaism in the synagogue. Rather, their synagogues blended into the cityscape, situated often in unidentified spaces, as had been the case for American Jews in both the colonial era and years of mass immigration.

Because of the centrality of the Lubavitcher Rebbe to his followers' lives, his Hasidim applied the Jewish religious concept of *daled amos*, or the four cubits of a Jew's home, to the Brooklyn neighborhood of Crown Heights. Thus they defined "the entire neighborhood as the Rebbe's home—a private Jewish space, and a uniquely holy place for his Hasidim." Unlike other charismatic rabbis, Schneerson led his followers from his home rather than from his synagogue, departing from one of the key features of American Judaism. Crown Heights stood at the heart of the Rebbe's worldwide effort to spread Hasidism, making it "nothing less than the spiritual center of the Jewish people," as anthropologist Henry Goldschmidt observes. "Crown Heights thus echoes, and to some extent supplants, the Holy Land of Israel" for the Lubavitchers.[93] In this framework, the sacred space of the synagogue matters very little in announcing the visible presence of Jews in cities across the United States. Synagogues for Hasidim are merely a place to pray, not institutions that herald American Judaism's urban origins. Instead a city neighborhood becomes potentially sacred space.

In the 1960s young American Jews who had often grown up in large suburban synagogues created a parallel movement in Jewish religious life to ecstatic Hasidic prayer. Inspired in part by Hasidic pietism, they sought intimacy, informality, and community in prayer through the creation of a *havurah* (fellowship). These loose-knit fellowships, whether established in Boston, New York, or Los Angeles, sometimes took the form of a prayer minyan, only now that feminism had transformed Judaism, most adopted a commitment to egalitarianism. Women sat in a circle together with men; they led prayers and read from the Torah scroll. A havurah might meet in apartments or private homes. As their popularity grew, synagogues also sponsored them, offering, as it were, the basement that Jewish immigrants had requested of Shearith Israel. Riv-Ellen Prell discovered in her ethnographic research on the Library Minyan (better than the basement) in Los Angeles "people healing wounds like those of my father and others of his generation who could not reconcile the Judaism of their parents and the American lives they sought." These groups of Jews "rejected the decorum and aesthetics of the parents' generation," she observed, while maintaining a commitment to "autonomy and expressive individualism" for Judaism in American culture. Thus cities nourished alternative and diverse Jewish religious practices, whether as a result of the arrival of Hasidic Holocaust survivors or through innovations by American-born Jews seeking new forms of spirituality different from the suburban Judaism of their youth.[94]

To end this chapter on a note of irony, the migrations of Jews into and

Building at 770 Eastern Parkway, headquarters and synagogue of Chabad Lubavitch Hasidim and model for Chabad buildings around the world. Courtesy Andrea Robbins and Max Becher and Sonnabend Gallery NYC.

out of American cities, and within cities, into and out of neighborhoods, led the elegant Crown Heights section of Brooklyn where the Brooklyn Jewish Center had been built to metamorphose in the 1960s into a lower-middle-class area filled with African Americans (mostly from the West Indies) and Hasidic Jews. As a result of these urban transformations in the 1970s the Brooklyn Jewish Center became an adjunct of Chabad, the Lubavitch outreach organization, which turned it into a school for boys. Chabad's central synagogue at 770 Eastern Parkway is a modern shtibl that accommodates the crowds of thousands who flock to attend services on Sabbaths and during holidays, an alternative to both the synagogue-center and large, formal civic synagogue buildings. "After purchasing the physician's office at 770," the scholar Maya Balakirsky Katz observes, "Chabad made no attempt to hide its original function as a medical clinic that performed illegal abortions; indeed, its previous life allowed the building, once sanctified, to achieve a greater measure of distance from its previous role to its present holy work."[95] Katz argues that architectural consecration rather than appropriation distinguishes Chabad's approach in the urban milieu.

The tripeaked, red brick home "signaled Chabad's revitalization in a country" that promised to be a final resting place for Lubavitch Hasidim before the coming of the Messiah. It came to represent a shift away from Eastern Europe to the American city, Chabad's divinely ordained home. Then, "in an unprecedented move in the mid-1980s," notes Katz, "the

Rebbe initiated a mission to replicate the Brooklyn shtibl; he directed his followers to build an exact replica in Israel as a satellite chapter." This decision "transformed Chabad from a dynastic leadership model to an international, corporate-style Jewish religious organization."[96]

As Chabad extended its efforts to reach Jews throughout the world, it exported its Brooklyn model. Schneerson saw 770, Chabad's world headquarters, as "the place to which the Messiah would come first and from which he would lead the return of the Jews from exile to the Holy Land." This radically new theological concept envisioned a Messiah coming to the world "by way of America."[97] The decision to incorporate the building and remove it from a private residence, designed in part to prevent any family members from making a claim on the property (the Rebbe and his wife had no children), led to its iteration as a potent symbol of Chabad's theology. It also transformed the dynastic court of house/shtibl into a building with both sanctity and collective attributes similar to a synagogue. "During the height of the property dispute in New York's federal court, the Rebbe urged his followers in the Israeli settlement Kfar Chabad to raise a building within the year, a request that inspired speculation on the imminent arrival of the Messiah." Once the court ruled in favor of the institutional model of ownership in 1987, Chabad embarked on a worldwide building program. As a result Chabad built replicas of 770 in such cities as Rio de Janeiro, Melbourne, and Buenos Aires and on the campus of Rutgers University in New Jersey, not to mention in Israel. Katz argues, "Chabad shifted its focus from what it saw as a failed Russian history to an optimistic and proudly American religious identity and, in this shift, and with an adeptness that could be seen as very modern, Chabad transformed its institutional identity from a Hasidic dynasty to a religious corporation."[98] American Judaism's urban origins now appear throughout the world as exemplary expressions of Lubavitch Hasidism heralding the imminent arrival of the Messiah.

CHAPTER 2

STREETS

On June 12, 1994, thousands of Jews gathered on the streets of Crown Heights to mourn the Lubavitcher Rebbe, Menachem Mendel Schneerson. They came to Brooklyn from across the United States, from Israel, and from all over the world for his funeral. A huge crowd of men, women, and children followed the plain pine coffin, many of them walking the ten miles to the cemetery in Queens. Gary Rosenblatt, editor of the New York *Jewish Week*, recalled sixteen years later how he could still hear the "sudden gasp, followed by a loud, spontaneous and mournful wail that erupted from the thousands gathered outside 770 Eastern Parkway in Brooklyn when the simple wooden casket carrying the remains of the Lubavitcher Rebbe, Menachem Mendel Schneerson, emerged from the movement's headquarters."[1]

For four decades, the Rebbe led his pious followers, his Hasidim, building a worldwide movement to reach Jews wherever they might be. Beginning in the 1960s and accelerating in subsequent decades, "this campaign sought to insert traditional Jewish religious behavior and more specifically concrete mitzvahs into the public square and onto the Jewish agenda. The importance of transforming the individual was at the core of every campaign."[2] Emissaries of Chabad Lubavitch fanned out around the world to ignite the holy spark of Jewishness in every Jew, inspiring thousands to perform a single commandment, a mitzvah, to hasten the messianic redemption. These commandments could be as simple as saying a prayer or putting on tefillin or, for women, lighting Sabbath candles and blessing them. Since they sought not to convert Jews but rather to use an inherent religious power that Jews possessed if they followed the commandments, the Lubavitch Hasidim urged action rather than faith. First the streets of New York and then those of many other cities staged encounters between Hasidim and other Jews. While the funeral marked the Rebbe's passing, his spirit has endured in compelling ways. His Chabad movement has grown into the largest, most successful, and well-funded international Jewish movement. By 2003 Chabad had mobilized four thousand representatives in seventy-six countries.[3]

Going public on the streets invited all urban residents to observe and consider Jews. Jewish behavior on city streets fell into two broad categories: moments of mobilization as with the funeral of the Rebbe and everyday engagements that extended ordinary Jewish ways of living and made them part of the American urban milieu. Chabad's mitzvah mobiles stood somewhere between these two modes of public Judaism since they did not draw huge crowds or disrupt regular patterns of urban life, nor did they become completely integrated into prosaic dimensions of the city. Chabad's innovations remind us of the manifold possibilities offered by city streets for religious experimentation. They suggest, too, a continuum of Jewish practices rather than a sharp divide. Thus Jewish public religious activity ranged from the mundane, which often appeared in commerce and daily and weekly rhythms of the streets, to the extraordinary, which happened at most once a year.

This chapter ponders examples of these practices mostly drawn from New York City in order to understand the particular power of urban streets to reinforce and modify American Judaism. It recognizes, as historian Richard Cohen argues, "public space was a venue in which Jews could give free rein" to their aspirations to create a public Judaism that would reflect their economic, cultural, and political strength.[4] This chapter traces a historical arc over the course of several centuries of patterns of Jewish behavior in the streets as well as moments of mobilization that demonstrated Jews' city presence.

American Judaism emerged from Jews' engagement with city streets and reflected their social, political, economic, and religious dimensions. Unlike the Italian street *festa* that temporarily established sacred parameters of a saint's domain, Jewish claims to city streets rested on more material grounds.[5] Streets were neither sacred nor secular. As permanent public spaces they appealed to Jews who claimed them for their politics. Streets amplified Jews' political opinions, whether expressed at corner rallies or through protest marches or boycotts. Streets also facilitated both ethnic cooperation and conflict. Battles over neighborhood turf, economic competition, and political control occurred on the city's streets. These contests possessed religious dimensions. Anti-Semitic incidents scarred the streets of large American cities when residents attacked Jewish shops and Jewish peddlers, who earned their living in public.

Religious observance resonated on streets since they served as thoroughfares on which Jews walked to the synagogue every Sabbath and holiday. Until the 1920s most Jews living in cities resided in neighborhoods that did not distinguish between residential and commercial areas, where Jewish-owned stores often lined the sidewalks. When these shops closed in honor of a Jewish holiday, their mute façades testified to Judaism's power and appeal. Conversely when they remained open they deliberately disregarded Jewish law requiring abstention from work on Sabbaths and holy days. Jewish shopkeepers thus signified Judaism's weakened attraction compared to the demands of Saturday business. Jews living in the neighborhood recognized the religious significance of these business decisions. Religious practice was not a private matter. It spilled over into city streets.

The Rebbe's funeral had important antecedents in Jewish use of the streets for public ceremonies. Ninety years before his death, the funeral of Rabbi Jacob Joseph initiated decades of massive Jewish funerals, extraordinary events that stopped traffic and attracted Christians' attention. In 1888 Rabbi Joseph had accepted the invitation of several Orthodox congregations on the Lower East Side to establish a chief rabbinate. His 1902 funeral offers both powerful similarities as well as striking differences to that of the Lubavitcher Rebbe. Tens of thousands turned out on July 30 to mourn Rabbi Joseph's death as they did for Schneerson; however, unlike the Rebbe's mourners, many who grieved at Rabbi Joseph's passing had scorned him in life.[6] Weeping and moaning, they followed the funeral cortege as it wound through the streets of Lower Manhattan en route to the cemetery in Brooklyn. Hundreds of boys walked in front of the coffin chanting psalms. Storekeepers closed their shops, and mechanics, laborers, and pushcart peddlers sacrificed a day's wages to attend the funeral. The police had not anticipated so many participants.

When the procession reached Grand Street, heading toward the Brooklyn ferry, it went by the massive building of the Hoe and Company printing press manufacturing factory. Most of its eighteen hundred workers were Irish. As the cortege passed beneath the factory windows, workers started to pelt the mourners with iron and screws, blocks of wood, and sheets of water from buckets. Although the casket reached the ferry safely, police officers arrived at the factory and immediately began clubbing the mourners. Over two hundred people required medical attention. "East Side Jews considered the behavior of the police during the riot not as an ephemeral outburst but as part of a systematic and persistent persecution," writes historian Leonard Dinnerstein. Given the preponderance of Irish policemen, he views the funeral and riot "in the context of developing antagonisms caused by an older and established ethnic group—the Irish—feeling overwhelmed and encroached upon by a newer one—the Jews—whose numbers appeared unlimited." Still, Dinnerstein characterizes the funeral as culminating in "the worst anti-Semitic police riot witnessed in America."[7]

Historian Arthur Goren considers Rabbi Joseph's funeral as one of the "rites of community" that New York Jews transposed from Old World to New. "Public funerals," he argues, "viewed as communal observances, were rituals of collective affirmation. They extended the boundaries of private grief and adoration—and often guilt—to embrace the kinship of community and nationality by celebrating the virtues of the fallen leader or mentor." Religious Jews used public funerals of important rabbis "to enhance their image among their own people and among the gentiles."[8] But they were not the only Jews to adopt funerals for such public purposes. Funeral processions demarcated the dimensions of Jewish New York.

Unlike daily usage of the streets that magnified the urban dimensions of American Judaism, periodical demands for extraordinary events briefly claimed the city's streets as sites of religious demonstration. Far more than the occasional synagogue dedication, funeral processions as well as protest marches, rallies, and other parades gave evidence of the city's heterogeneity and multireligious character. As "public dramas of social relations," they drew on religious and political ideologies and agendas.[9] Christians watched these examples of Jewish public religious culture, they commented on them in the press, and occasionally they mobilized in opposition. Then the streets became potential battlegrounds as Jews sought to impress their religious and political agendas on the larger urban world.

Goren notes how changes occurred in New York City, where Jews who no longer cared about rabbis or felt guilty about their lack of religious piety turned to massive public funerals to memorialize their new cultural heroes. In 1909 the famous Yiddish playwright Jacob Gordin received a mammoth funeral procession. "Hold this day sacred," urged the Yiddish daily *Forverts*. "Gather together at his grave. . . . Bring wreaths of flowers with you." As Goren observes, "The summons to escort a revered figure to his grave was, of course, in keeping with age-old practice. Bringing wreaths of flowers was not." Traditional Jewish custom considered efforts to provide pleasure at a funeral, such as would come from flowers, inappropriate at a time of mourning. But Gordin's funeral departed in important ways from traditional Jewish practices, borrowing more than flowers from Christians. At the memorial meeting in the Thalia Theater, the open coffin revealed his embalmed body, contrary to Jewish law. The Yiddish poet Morris Rosenfeld (1862–1923) commented, "When all the eulogies and lamentations were over, people didn't want to leave the theater. An inner feeling drew them to the stage. One wanted to cheer and shout the familiar—'Gordin, bravo Gordin.'" Outside vendors hawked buttons with his picture, a commercial endeavor popularized when the archbishop had died.[10]

Perhaps the most outrageous of the public funerals was that of October 1912 honoring Big Jack Zelig (William Alberts), a gangster. Zelig's claim to fame rested on his "defense" of the Jewish Lower East Side neighborhood from depredations by other immigrants. He fought the Irish and the Italians, though mostly to defend his own turf. He wanted to shake down Lower East Side Jewish merchants, collect "protection money," and run gambling and prostitution rings without interference from members of other ethnic groups. When he was murdered at twenty-four, his confederates opted for a big procession, hiring a leading funeral director to arrange a stately service with yeshiva students to say psalms and a procession of twenty-five automobiles and thirty-six carriages. "To top it off," observes Goren, they interred the reputed "chief of New York's underworld" in a place of honor between Jacob Gordin's grave and that of a famous rabbi. In this case these religious rites testified to the corruption of the streets rather than their sanctification. In the old country Zelig would have received a "donkey's funeral" and interment outside the cemetery fence, a mark of disgrace. In America, it seemed, religious honor could be purchased.[11]

Sholem Aleichem (Solomon Rabinovich, 1859–1916) satirized the American Jewish way of death in a short story published a few years after Zelig's funeral. In "Beryl Isaac and the Wonders of America," Aleichem's skeptical interlocutor queries, "Don't people die in America?" Of course they do, he's told, but how they die and, more important, how they're buried are wonderful. Beryl Isaac goes on to describe what happens when a rich man dies. Such a funeral costs a thousand dollars, a stupendous sum.

> Outside, the sun shines and the weather is magnificent. The coffin is placed on a black bier trimmed with silver. The horses wear black pompons with white feathers. And the clergy—rabbis, cantors, reverends—are all dressed in black with white buttons. Carriages galore follow the coffin and children from the talmud torah schools walk ahead singing out loud: "Righteousness shall go before Him, And shall make his footsteps a way." The singing is heard throughout the city.
>
> By contrast, if one doesn't have so much money, the funeral lacks a certain panache. The second class funeral costs only five hundred dollars. The day is not as bright. The coffin is also placed on a black platform but without the silver trimming. The horses and members of the clergy wear black but without feathers and without white buttons.

Needless to say, no singing of psalms reverberates throughout the city.

But pity the working-class man. He cannot afford much. His funeral costs "only one hundred dollars. The weather is cool and overcast. There is no bier, only two horses, and only two members of the clergy." As for the poor man, his funeral costs not a cent. "No ceremonies, no sign of horses or members of the clergy. Outside is a downpour of rain. Two reverends are on both sides and in the middle is the corpse. The three drag themselves on foot to the cemetery."[12]

Sholem Aleichem's own funeral was even greater than the one he satirized. New York Jews truly exploited the power inherent in a funeral's religious drama when the famous Yiddish writer died. On May 15, 1916, the procession slowly made its way from his home in the Bronx down through Harlem and the East Side of Manhattan along Fifth and Madison Avenues, and then wended through the Lower East Side before crossing the Williamsburg Bridge to the Brooklyn cemetery. Estimates put the crowds between a hundred thousand and a quarter of a million, with thousands watching from windows, fire escapes, and rooftops.

Multiple stops along the way for funeral orations highlighted the importance of Yiddish culture and brought attention to those Jewish organizations chosen to eulogize the popular writer, a true culture hero. These stops addressed religious practice, self-government, education, and charity.[13] Their drama portrayed Aleichem as a Jewish "icon." His was the largest funeral procession New Yorkers had ever seen, lasting from nine o'clock in the morning until four thirty in the afternoon. As the scholar Ellen Kellman notes, "The innovative structure and symbolic elements employed by the funeral planners denoted an attempt on their part to adapt Jewish death ritual to the new and unfamiliar terrain of big city America, and in so doing to affirm the size, strength, and civility of the New York Jewish community before the whole city." In truth, the familiarity of New York Jews with the city's many dimensions contributed to the success of the funeral procession, which passed through exactly the right neighborhoods in three boroughs on its way to the cemetery. Kellman concludes that New York Jews, in mourning Sholom Aleichem, assumed an identity of "*goles* [exiled] Jews. Traversing the Jewish turf of their adopted city, they mourned the Yiddish writer as one vast community of the uprooted."[14] Ironically the uprootedness of exile—a theological concept and cultural condition—facilitated Jews' ability to sink new roots in the city's rich urban soil.

Funerals provide a fascinating glimpse not only into Jewish uses of the streets for extraordinary occasions but also into Jewish responses to urban pressures, that is, they reveal both the special and the mundane effects of cities on American Judaism. Although massive Jewish funeral processions largely disappeared by World War II, the growth of an American Jewish funeral industry owed its origins to the demands of urban life. Thus ordinary dimensions of Jewish religious ritual acquired new forms in urban America.

Traditionally Jews allocated responsibility for burying the dead to a voluntary association, *hevra kadisha* (Holy Association), that ritually washed and dressed the body (*tahara*), prepared the simple pine coffin (when coffins were required for burial), and escorted the body to the cemetery. Membership in the hevra kadisha usually was reserved for communal leaders; men cared for men and women cared for women. Jews established cemeteries at the city's edges since Judaism required the dead to be buried beyond residential areas. Often the purchase of land for a cemetery preceded the organization of a congregation in a city. The dead needed a place to rest among Jews; the living could live among non-Jews. (Another way to consider this: a quorum of ten Jews was mandated for communal prayer, but only one dead Jew required a Jewish cemetery.)

But as American cities grew, the distances between where Jews lived—and died—and where they were buried increased so that by the late nineteenth century Jews had to hire transportation to take their dead for burial. Communal practices that had taken care of interment struggled to keep up with a burgeoning Jewish population. More and more people died in hospitals, necessitating two trips: first to take the corpse home and then to the cemetery. The undertaker, a "species of middleman made necessary by the complexities of the modern city," gradually superseded the traditional burial society.[15]

At this point, enterprising Jewish deliverymen and undertakers realized that they could expand their business if they offered additional services. Jews rejected embalming, which swept the United States as a result of the Civil War. Nor did they care for cremation. But crowded tenement apartments made purifying a corpse difficult, even with the requirement of immediate burial, usually within twenty-four hours. In addition, modern bureaucracy requiring registration of deaths spurred specialization. So the deliverymen and undertakers teamed up and assumed these tasks. They handled the city-mandated details, removed the corpse to a funeral "parlor" (a commercial version of a home), prepared and clothed the body according to Jewish ritual, and provided transportation to the cemetery. Soon they were offering additional funeral "services," including a religious functionary to read psalms and give a eulogy.[16]

By the mid-twentieth century, several generations of American Jews had come to accept these commercialized and privatized funeral practices as traditional. Jewish undertakers evolved into funeral directors and established a number of large chains of urban funeral homes. In 1932 Jews formed the Jewish Funeral Directors Association of America in a bid to upgrade their status. Handling Jewish deaths in American cities became a big, albeit family, business. (In fact, the enterprising son of one funeral director realized that he could make use of the limousines that replaced carriages in the 1920s by repurposing them in the evenings for revelers at weddings and other occasions, thus giving rise to a rental car business.) Only in the late twentieth century did a small movement of Jews seek to return to a communal alternative of the hevra kadisha.[17]

City streets were sites of celebration as well as mourning, of protest as well as conflict. Through religious displays, "urban people announced in their own voices the heterogeneity of the city."[18] Religious practices as much as politics fueled claims by immigrants to join national debates about pluralism, multiculturalism, and heterogeneity. These religious differences, coupled with ethnic competition for jobs and housing as well as pressures from international events, on occasion inflamed city streets. In many large American cities, both Jews and Irish Catholics struggled to claim the streets, to announce and secure their presence in the city. Although these groups would gradually cease to compete with each other in the years after World War II, Jewish conflict with other religious and ethnic groups in the city emerged instead.[19] One of the most vivid clashes between two "chosen peoples" with different religious worldviews erupted on the streets of Brooklyn in the late twentieth century.

Almost a hundred years after the riot at Rabbi Jacob Joseph's funeral, on a Monday evening in August 1991, Menachem Mendel Schneerson, the Lubavitcher Rebbe, was returning to his office on Eastern Parkway from a visit to the cemetery where his father was buried. The Rebbe did not travel alone. He received a police escort; his motorcade also included a station wagon carrying members of his staff. As the wagon crossed the intersection of Utica Avenue and President Street, a car heading north on Utica struck it. The wagon careened onto the sidewalk, where Gavin Cato, a seven-year-old boy from Guyana, was learning with his cousin how to ride a bike. Both children were crushed and gravely wounded. Emergency vehicles rushed to the site of the accident, as did police. An ambulance sponsored by Orthodox Jews arrived first, followed by one from New York's Emergency Medical Services. The latter treated the critically injured children on the spot while the former took the driver and occupants of the wagon to the hospital. But Gavin Cato died before reaching the hospital.

Soon a crowd of African Americans gathered at the corner, upset at the death and the perceived unequal treatment of Jews and Blacks. Within an hour, angry rhetoric and shouts of "Get the Jews!" filled the air. Hundreds ran west toward Kingston Avenue, the Jewish shopping street. Some threw rocks and bottles, broke windows, burned cars. Around eleven twenty on the corner of President Street and Brooklyn Avenue, five long blocks from the site of the fatal accident, they encountered Yankel Rosenbaum, a twenty-nine-year-old orthodox Jew from Australia who was living in Crown Heights and conducting research for his doctoral dissertation. The crowd surrounded him, punching and kicking him. The police arrived within minutes, but as they did, Lemrick Nelson, a sixteen-year-old born in Brooklyn to immigrant parents from Trinidad, pulled a pocketknife and stabbed Rosenbaum four times in the back and torso. Although taken to the hospital, Rosenbaum died from his wounds.[20]

For the next two days and nights, riots tore through the neighborhood of Crown Heights, home to the Lubavitcher Rebbe and many Hasidim, home as well to thousands of Afro-Caribbean immigrants and their children, who made up the majority population. Police mobilized but seemed unable to stop young men from throwing bottles and rocks at each other. Only on the third day did police finally quell the violence and an uneasy truce settled over the neighborhood's streets.

Since the 1970s and 1980s, Crown Heights has hosted two competing communities, one Jewish, one Afro-Caribbean. Although they share the blocks and even live in adjoining apartments, members of each community have relatively little contact with each other. Each Labor Day, as many as a million people pour into the neighborhood for the Annual West Indian parade up Eastern Parkway, a tribute to Afro-Caribbean music and culture. And each year, on the Jewish holiday of Simhat Torah (Rejoicing in the Torah), thousands of Hasidim fill the streets around 770 Eastern Parkway to celebrate. Both groups recognize how the streets enlarge their presence and produce meaning; both understand how social space is contested terrain that can enhance or reduce their power.

The events of August 1991 represent one of the most violent attacks on Jews in their history in the United States. Although riots and gang fights occurred throughout the nineteenth and twentieth centuries, pitting Jews against other groups in the city—especially Irish, Italian, and African American (in fact the musical *West Side Story* that recasts Shakespeare's *Romeo and Juliet* into a street story of warring gangs originally was imagined as East Side Story with Jews fighting Italians)[21]—the years since World War II had been remarkably free of such violence.

The return of street conflict produced two contested narratives of what had happened. For African Americans the issues revolved around race and racism, structural inequalities that produced a child's death from an auto accident. By contrast Jews dubbed the events a "pogrom," that is, a form of state-sanctioned anti-Semitic violence directed against Jews because they are Jews. From their perspective what happened in Crown Heights related not to urban violence in Detroit, or Los Angeles, or Newark as it did for blacks, but rather to attacks on Jews in such Russian cities as Kishinev or Odessa. Each group imagined a different history. One privileged the lingering effects of the original violence of slavery in the United States while the other remembered the lachrymose history of Jewish suffering in Europe. As anthropologist Henry Goldschmidt argues, the operative categories for Jews were religious, not racial. Narratives of "riot" versus "pogrom" both "establish powerful continuities between past and present—continuities that are defined by, while simultaneously defining, the fundamental nature of Blackness and Jewishness."[22]

City streets play a central role as space in which to stage understandings of Jewish identity, whether these understandings emerge out of rites of community or forms of public culture or whether they come from everyday behaviors or even occasional fights. "Urban street life is a spectacle of recognizable signs," the scholar of religion Robert Orsi observes, "a semiotics of place that divides the initiated from the uninitiated." One of the distinguishing features of cities is their promiscuity, mixing those in the know with newcomers. Jews in America quickly became city people, adept at decoding performative street language. Orsi contends, "style is so important to urban people and to urban religion" because it distinguishes one group from another. Through, in other words, "the intricate intentionalities of public self-representation, and especially through style in religion," city folk make meanings and impress those meanings on themselves and others, especially when they live at the "borders and junctures of adjacent urban social worlds."[23]

One of the earliest efforts to produce both religious meaning and political authority by marching through the streets of the city occurred in Philadelphia on July 4, 1788, when the city held a grand parade to celebrate Pennsylvania's ratification of the new Constitution. Philadelphia's Jews lined up to walk alongside their fellow countrymen. Gershom Mendes Seixas, who served as leader (hazzan) of Philadelphia's Mikveh Israel congregation (and later would return to New York City as head of Shearith Israel), marched at the front of the parade, linking arms with clergy of the different Christian denominations. His visibility inspired observers to reflect on the religious tolerance of the new nation evident in its willingness to include non-Christians in such a public patriotic event. The United States, the parade apparently proclaimed, welcomed Jews as part of its civic and religious democracy.

At the parade's end, the weary but exuberant marchers were treated to tables of food, including a kosher table for the Jews. While the marchers undoubtedly appreciated the meal, historians have debated how to interpret this event. Did the kosher table point to recognition of Jews' differences and a willingness to accept them? Did Jews march as Americans and dine as Jews? Or did the kosher table symbolize the impossibility of assimilating Jews? Did their separation at the parade's end indicate their desire to remain apart? Or perhaps the parade symbolically testified to the ideal of religious equality. Such questions about Jewish differences and similarities from other Americans have reverberated throughout the nineteenth and twentieth centuries, made more compelling by the visible presence of Jews and their Judaism on city streets. The Philadelphia parade inaugurated a new way of thinking about American Jews, incorporating their religious representative at the head of the parade and respecting their religious practices at its conclusion.[24]

The Fourth of July parade may have been the first one to include Jews prominently as equal American citizens despite their rejection of Christianity, but it was hardly the last. As urban residents, Jews rarely failed to participate in important parades through town. They joined in the massive funeral parade held in New York City that followed Abraham Lincoln's casket in 1865; they celebrated the 1876 centennial in parades in Philadelphia and other cities; they marched in Chicago with union members in Labor Day parades and with fellow political radicals on May Day, boldly carrying banners in Yiddish. Annual Labor Day parades and May Day rallies signaled Jews' sense of solidarity with U.S. workers and with an international proletariat. Jewish participation in parades as Jews, usually distinguished by their signs, spoke to their civic consciousness as well as their politics. In fact, their exclusion from certain parades—such as those for Mardi Gras in New Orleans—often signified their separateness from the city's civic life. When Jews finally won the opportunity late in the twentieth century to form a krewe to join the parade, they did so despite its explicitly Catholic roots.[25]

Cities fostered cooperation as well as conflict, visible not only in moments of mobilization but also in everyday engagements. Jews' daily use of the streets transformed some of them into ordinary Jewish spaces. As newcomers to American cities Jews often demonstrated a willingness to adopt different ways of living, as the evolution of their American funeral rituals reveals. Many saw in cities opportunities to develop a wide range of Jewish religious practices and build Judaism into flourishing and ever-changing cityscapes. They perceived a chance to craft a multireligious urban milieu and to influence the shape of metropolitan growth. From the early colonial port cities through the raw new cities of the prairies in the nineteenth century to the booming industrial cities of the twentieth century, urban areas have provided more than locales for American Judaism. They have given Judaism urban roots and city smarts, making Jews public figures and allowing them to establish through their everyday neighborhood practices a handful of prominent Jewish places.

Urban religion of necessity exists on city streets, and Jews have often endowed their local streets with rhythms drawn from the Jewish calendar. How religious groups understand streets and how they incorporate them into a religious worldview have varied across time. As cities change, so do religious attitudes and practices of urban residents. "City folk do not live *in* their environments; they live *through* them," argues Orsi. "Who am I? What is possible in life? What is good? These are questions that are always asked." They are, he indicates, religious questions, not specifically urban ones. But they are answered in the city as much as anywhere else. As "men and women cobble together responses, they act upon spaces in transformative ways."[26] Jewish answers to those questions shaped urban neighborhoods and, eventually, the larger city itself. In seeking to live each day through their environment, Jews adopted responses to changing American cities. Those responses varied, however, producing inherently pluralist milieus.

Judaism required observances that altered urban spaces, with the result that Jews periodically crafted Jewish places out of ordinary commercial, residential, and industrial streets. Some Jewish places endured for decades, redolent of Jewish ways of acting in the world; others disappeared as Jews moved through cities. When thousands of Jews left cities for suburbs in the decades after World War II, the rate of disappearance increased. Formerly Jewish places reverted to urban spaces, leaving behind residues of a Jewish presence. Then buildings facing the streets acquired a patina, a kind of palimpsest hinting at lived realities of previous generations. That absence endured until Jews excavated their past.

This process of imprinting city streets with a Jewish religious presence began in the eighteenth century, although it accelerated in the nineteenth and twentieth centuries. Yet even in the early years of Jewish settlement in British colonial seaports, Jews manifested their existence on the streets just by going about their regular observance of the Sabbath. "A resident of New York standing outside the newly constructed Mill Street synagogue in the 1730s could not have missed the arrival of Lewis Gomez, one of the city's wealthiest Jewish merchants," writes Howard Rock in his history of New York Jews. "The family marched in procession, led by the elder Gomez. Following them were his personal slaves carrying the family's prayer books and prayer shawls. In a ceremony symbolic of the deferential nature of colonial American society, upon reaching the synagogue the slaves entered, placed the books and shawls on the proper chairs and left as the family took their seats."[27]

Rock's account demonstrates not only how Judaism appeared very early on the streets of New York but also how American social practices shaped Jewish observances. Unless there was an *eruv* or boundary marker demarcating public spaces as collectively Jewish and private, Jews were forbidden to carry items outside their homes during the Sabbath. However, non-Jews could carry for them.[28] In this case, Gomez used his slaves to carry the religious articles needed for prayer despite the biblical injunction that slaves were also to rest on the Sabbath.

No "Jewish street" existed in the American colonies as in Europe. Neither were there ghettoes as in Italy or *mellahs* as in North African cities, urban areas to which Jews were confined at night.[29] Instead Jews in North America lived on blocks not far from their synagogues or built their synagogues near the streets where they lived. As cities grew, Jews often moved to new sections with better housing, farther away from their synagogue. Those residential choices in turn necessitated either transporting the congregation to a locale closer to their homes or building another synagogue nearby since Jews needed to live within walking distance of their synagogue.

Jews rarely opted to stay close to a synagogue and forgo physical and social mobility. Torah scrolls were portable. Unlike some urban Catholics who preferred to not to leave their parish boundaries, Jews do not seem to have evinced sufficiently strong sentimental attachments to their synagogue buildings to maintain homes in the area. As sociologist Gerald Gamm notes, Jews paid relatively few penalties for moving; they were, after all, living in exile no matter whether the house was plain or fancy. Although they gave up an investment in bricks and mortar, they retained their congregations and often managed to relocate their synagogues. Gamm also argues that religious leadership by wealthy Jews, who tended to be among the first to move to a new neighborhood, propelled Jewish physical mobility, leaving the poor behind.[30]

When coupled with the growth of Jewish population in cities, this pattern of spatial mobility eventually distributed Jews along class lines. More prosperous Jews gravitated to middle- and upper-class neighborhoods; working-class Jews, poor Jews, and those in the lower middle class resided in modest sections, or in slums. As tens of thousands of Jews moved into burgeoning cities, they began to cluster according to ethnicity as well, with Russian Jews, for example, living in one subsection of a neighborhood and Romanian Jews in another and Hungarian

Jews in a third and Syrian Jews in a fourth. Yet despite this differentiation and pluralism, common features of public Judaism united Jewish urban areas.[31]

Jews initially left their religious imprint on city streets through commerce. King Street in Charleston, Chatham Square in New York City, Maxwell Street in Chicago, Decatur Street in Atlanta, Chene Street in Detroit—all of these retail streets contained mixtures of religions and ethnicities. But visible Jewish commercial activity attracted other Jews and usually provided connections to sustain religious life. Jewish newcomers to New York City in the years before the Civil War discovered that "Newman Cowen's Canal Street glass warehouse doubled as a charitable distribution site at the beginning of each Jewish month."[32] Commerce not only fueled religiously inspired charity but also formed the core of a Jewish residential neighborhood since Jews often lived behind or above their stores. This was the case in Atlanta in the nineteenth century, as well as in Cleveland, Pittsburgh, and Detroit in the twentieth century. Not until they achieved a modicum of economic security could Jews afford the luxury of living apart from where they earned their livelihood.[33]

As Jewish immigration mushroomed in the years after the Civil War and urban congestion complicated retail trade, many Jews sought possibilities for peddling within cities. Rather than circulating in the countryside for a week or two at a time as they had typically done in Europe and in the United States prior to the Civil War, they took some of the principles of peddling—small-scale commerce requiring little or no outlay of funds and producing extremely modest profits—into the streets. Pushcarts, rented for a few cents a day or acquired for a few dollars a year for a license, soon began to appear in Jewish sections of cities. These areas, characterized by mixed residential, industrial, and commercial uses, were located close to wholesale distribution points, near warehouses on the rivers in New York or by the railroads in Chicago.

In New York, the density of Jewish and Italian neighborhoods "supported the transition of street marketing from an occupation restricted to a small number of itinerant peddlers to an established retail institution." These pushcart vendors did not rove up and down the blocks of a neighborhood but stationed themselves in front of shops where they "developed a steady clientele of housewives."[34] They made certain Lower

East Side residential streets synonymous with shopping, first acquiring renown in the latter decades of nineteenth century: Hester Street (1886), Grand Street (1893), Orchard Street (1898), Rivington Street (1898). Pushcart peddlers endowed these streets with visible evidence of Jewish religious and ethnic difference and transformed these blocks into storied Jewish sites of immigrant life. Pushcarts sustained important urban Jewish practices even as they introduced innovations in American Judaism.

Pushcart peddlers complemented the rise of urban department stores, many owned by Jews, which similarly grouped different types of items for sale, albeit under a single roof rather than spread out along the street. Peddlers sold almost anything in small quantities: fruit and vegetables, fish and eggs, clothing and notions, pots and pans. Tenement apartments lacked storage space and iceboxes, so shopping involved almost daily trips to purchase food. Street vendors catered to these needs. However, they clashed repeatedly with police (another case of Irish-Jewish conflict) who harassed them, fined them, and often forced them to move on. Yet eventually peddlers won the right to remain stationary on the streets. Historian Daniel Bluestone argues that bans on street selling "sought to accommodate a vision of streets as exclusive travel arteries" and as such pointed to efforts to eclipse "earlier social uses of the street for political activity, gregarious socializing, and popular amusements."[35]

In New York peddling as an occupation attracted a significant minority of Jewish immigrants living on the Lower East Side. Peddling became a legitimate business and even a vehicle of upward mobility for some immigrant Jews. Historian Andrew Heinze argues that Jews "usually spent about five or six years on the streets and then invested their savings in an enterprise of their own." Pushcarts offered competitive prices and "catered to consumers who had been excluded from the burgeoning retail trade of America."[36]

Peddlers facilitated the emergence of new urban Jewish religious practices driven by American consumption patterns. By making products that were unavailable in Europe cheap and accessible, peddlers promoted consumption that encouraged Jews to Americanize. Abraham Cahan (1860–1951), the famous editor of the Yiddish daily *Forverts*, recounted this process in his immigrant novel, *The Rise of David Levinsky*. Not only does Levinsky ascend from rags to riches, but he also adopts methods of manufacturing cheap clothing. Just as department stores used such Christian holidays as Christmas and Easter to sell goods, Jewish merchants and peddlers urged Jews to enrich their observance of sacred days by buying special foods and clothes associated with the holiday. Despite these connections, Heinze argues, "the old role of luxuries as a symbol of earthly holiness collapsed under the pressure of city life."[37] When luxuries rarely associated with poor immigrant neighborhoods appeared on the streets in pushcarts, they acquired new meanings. Rather than earthly holiness they symbolized Jewish American abundance.

Such commerce produced visible versions of Judaism as an urban way of life, forms of Jewish lived religion.[38] Jews fulfilled their religious obligations by purchasing kosher food and ordering their lives according to the Jewish calendar. Regular prayer, membership in a congregation, and participation in worship services might enhance religious consciousness, but many Jews eschewed them. Instead they took note of holy days and Sabbaths at home or on the street. They also enthusiastically celebrated life-cycle events, such as weddings and bar mitzvahs. On the Lower East Side and in Jewish immigrant neighborhoods in other large cities like Chicago, stores geared their advertising to Jewish religious practices. They promoted bar mitzvah suits and ritual items, such as prayer books and prayer shawls, fostering new forms of American Judaism.

Jews adopted urban consumption patterns often in response to Christian behavior. A holiday such as Hanukkah began to flourish in the United States as a time for gifts because of its closeness to the Christmas shopping season. Passover, which coincided with Easter and spring fashions, heralded a frenzy of spring cleaning to accommodate its extensive requirements of ridding the house of all traces of leaven. As Jews gained a foothold in America, they gradually embraced American consumerism as part of their Passover preparations. So they not only cleaned thoroughly but also disposed of old dishes and pots and purchased new ones, which they would use first for the eight days of the holiday and subsequently for the rest of the year. Anyone walking the streets of the Lower East Side in the weeks before Pesach would have found them filled with discarded crockery, utensils, and even furniture.

In cities across the United States, Jews established kosher butcher shops and bakeries as well as "appetizing stores" and delicatessens to cater to Jewish immigrants' tastes. These forms of commerce fulfilled Jewish religious requirements to observe kashrut by separating meat and milk even as they elaborated on Jewish food customs. Appetizing stores, for example, an American urban innovation, specialized in dairy products such as cheeses as well as smoked fish, which as a neutral (or *parve*) food could accompany dairy items. By contrast delicatessens, another type of store elaborated by Jewish immigrants, served meat. Both types of stores featured rye bread, a Jewish favorite. Thus kosher practices became integral to urban culture, so much so that Woody Allen would later draw laughs with a deli scene in *Annie Hall* when Annie inappropriately orders pastrami on white bread with mayonnaise.

Yet food also provoked conflict, especially when prices rose unconscionably. Then streets became sites of mobilization as Jewish women recognized their power as consumers. In August 1892, after a butcher trust formed in the North End of Boston to fix prices for kosher food, a mass meeting of angry consumers, many of them women, gathered in synagogues to protest, "accusing the butchers who had agreed to fix prices of selling non-kosher meat." But they did not elicit much sympathy. As William Braverman wrote, the *Jewish Chronicle*, the local English-language weekly, "attacked the complaining Jews, noting that the same tactics had been employed in an attempt to reduce the price for killing fowl. Each consumer, the paper pointed out, had the option of buying her food from whatever dealer she chose, and there was no reason to embarrass the community with hysterical accusations."[39]

A decade later a more successful protest occurred in New York. In May 1902 married Jewish women instigated a boycott of kosher meat when the price doubled from eight to sixteen cents a pound. Their militancy shocked staid observers. The *New York Times* called for police repression of this "dangerous class" of women who "mostly speak a foreign language. . . . It will not do," the editorial admonished, "to have a swarm of ignorant and infuriated women going about any part of this city with petroleum destroying goods and trying to set fire to the shops of those against whom they are angry." These Jewish women did indeed stage their protest on the streets of their neighborhood. Mobilizing their neighbors against the depredations of the "Beef Trust," they not only prevented women from entering the many butcher shops on the Lower East Side but also boldly lifted the tops of pots being carried to the communal ovens filled with the Sabbath stew and poked to see that no meat lay buried beneath the vegetables. If they found meat, they flung it into the streets. After the first day when riots broke out, the women organized regular pickets in front of the butcher shops. The boycott soon spread to Harlem, the Bronx, and Brooklyn.[40]

Then on Saturday the women took their agitation to the synagogues. These determined women interrupted the reading of the Torah scroll because a matter of justice was at stake. They knew that they could stop the Sabbath worship service until their demands were heard. They sought the support of rabbis and male worshippers, especially husbands, to promise not to eat meat until the price came down. Most received a warm welcome, but in one synagogue the men called the police, objecting to the chutzpah of Mrs. Silver speaking from the bima. However, when the police moved to arrest her, a congregant "rose to compare the woman to the prophet Zachariah." His persuasion convinced the policeman to release her. On Sunday, anticipating a long struggle, the women established an organization, the Ladies Anti-Beef Trust Association, and began to reach out to Christian women for help.[41]

The historian Paula Hyman argues that the boycott, in addition to revealing the intersection of women's political activism and religious commitments, drew its strength from the urban neighborhood. "Rooted in the neighborhood, where many activities were quasi-public rather than strictly private, housewives were able to exert moral (as well as physical) suasion upon the women whom they saw on a daily basis." Significantly she argues, "They assumed the existence of collective goals and the right to demand shared sacrifices. Individual desires for the consumption of meat were to be subordinated to the larger public good." The women articulated a progressive urban vision of Jewish justice. When they were arrested, they remained defiant. "Did you throw meat on the street?" a judge asked Rose Peskin. "Certainly," she answered. "I should have looked it in the teeth?" After three weeks the price finally dropped.[42]

Surrounded by other Jews going about their daily activities in such crowded urban neighborhoods, Jews lived Jewish American lives. The Yiddish signs, the languages on the streets, and of course the people all radiated a Jewish ethos. Judaism on such streets was a lived religion, its everyday practices shaped by ordinary Jews. The streets regularly reminded Jews of their Judaism because they magnified Jewish practices, whether those stemmed from specific religious strictures, such as foods to eat, or reflected collective experiences, such as Yiddish cultural productions or Jewish politics.

Jewish time shaped the rhythm of the streets. Although many Jews went to work on the Sabbath since they could ill afford not to toil on what was considered a work day in America, the streets still assumed a quieter air. The Yiddish poet I. J. Schwartz, who settled in Lexington, Kentucky, in 1918, wrote with a touch of pathos about the contradictions of laboring on the Sabbath in southern cities where Jewish stores often catered to African Americans.

The joke was

> That one worked on the Sabbath
> Even harder than on the week-day,
> Because on Saturday people got their wages;
> They fitted shoes and pants on Negroes,
> And talked their hearts out—
> But as soon as the stars appeared,
> The merchant immediately stopped his business,
> Withdrew quickly behind the partition
> And said the *Havdoleh* out loud.[43]

Thus Jewish merchants marked the ritual end of the Sabbath at evening and said the prayers dividing sacred from profane time, despite their desecration of the Sabbath prohibition against work.

Street commerce boosted certain Jewish religious patterns while weakening others. Sabbath observance, perhaps the most important Jewish religious practice, suffered terribly. Most Jewish men and unmarried women went to work on Saturdays, violating the Sabbath, because they needed to earn a livelihood. Even though they usually worked for Jewish employers, they could not get the day off since Sunday was adopted by the states as the official day of rest. Still the streets reflected reduced commercial activity as some peddlers and shop owners closed their establishments to honor the Sabbath.

Ironically the spirit of the Sabbath pervaded the public atmosphere especially on Thursdays and Friday mornings when housewives did their shopping in preparation. Married Jewish women retained home rituals on Friday evenings. They would usher in the Sabbath by lighting and blessing candles and preparing a special meal that included *challah*, a braided white bread, as well as fish and meat. In his postwar memoir *A Walker in the City* (1951), Alfred Kazin writes about waiting outside in the rain on a London street where he heard a radio broadcast of the first Sabbath service at the Bergen Belsen concentration camp. "When the liberated Jewish prisoners recited the *Hear O Israel, the Lord Our God, the Lord is One*, I felt myself carried back to the Friday evenings at home, when with the Sabbath at sundown a healing quietness would come over Brownsville."[44]

The memory summoned up for Kazin a vision of the Brooklyn neighborhood. "It was the darkness and emptiness of the streets I liked most about Friday evening, as if in preparation for that day of rest and worship which the Jews greet 'as a bride'—that day when the very touch of money is prohibited, all work, all travel, all household duties, even to the turning on and off of a light—Jewry had found its way past its tormented heart to some ancient still center of itself. I waited," he admitted, "for the streets to go dark on Friday evening as other children waited for the Christmas lights." Kazin linked the public neighborhood world with the intimacy of his apartment. "Even Friday morning," he recalled, ". . . glowed in anticipation. When I returned home after three, the warm odor of a coffee cake baking in the oven and the sight of my mother on her hands and knees scrubbing the linoleum on the dining room floor filled me with such tenderness that I could feel my senses reaching out to embrace every single object in our household."[45]

On the high holy days of Rosh Hashanah and Yom Kippur, a tangible mood of reverence pervaded Jewish immigrant neighborhoods because commerce ground to a halt, children skipped school, and most Jews attended worship services. But in the fall before the high holy days immigrant Jewish neighborhoods hummed with commerce. Stores ran specials on clothing for men, women, and children; bakeries offered fancy round challah loaves, the shape auguring life's wholeness. The New Year meant a time for a fresh start, for repentance and renewal. In cities throughout America where Jews lived it also meant an occasion for new clothes, which would then be worn during the rest of the year. That the Jewish New Year coincided with both the start of the public school year and the arrival of the fall fashion shopping season enhanced its importance. Jews drew on these coincidences of Jewish ritual time with American public institutions and a consumer economy to strengthen their own urban Judaism.

Private personal reminiscences demonstrate how much these intertwined ways of observing Judaism entered a child's consciousness. In the early 1960s Samuel Golden dictated his memoirs of growing up on the Lower East Side, living next door to a stable whose smell and flies pervaded the hot tenement apartment every summer. Like many Jewish parents Golden's father bought him a new suit for the high holy days. It was "an annual event of the greatest significance."[46]

These Jewish practices reached the consciousness of Christian New Yorkers, some of whom took advantage of their knowledge to torment Jews. When Golden was eight or nine years old, "dressed up and on my way for the first evening service of Rosh Hashanah ushering in the new year holiday," he had to cross Cherry Street to get from his apartment to the synagogue. "On this particular night, a group of boys out for a little fun, surrounded me. As I looked around, it seemed as if every one of the boys had an egg in his hand. They didn't throw any at me. They just tried to slip eggs into all of my pockets—on the right side and the left side, the vest pocket and any pocket they could get at. As soon as they had shoved several eggs into my pockets, they began smacking and slapping at the pockets until they were sure that the eggs were completely crushed. You can imagine," Golden recalled, "what it meant to wait for the Rosh Hashanah holy days to get a suit, only to have it ruined before you even were able to show it to everybody in the synagogue! When they left me, my pockets were dripping. Instead of proceeding to the synagogue, I tearfully ran back home."[47]

Such an account depicts Jewish vulnerability in cities where the potential for conflict with other urban religious groups tarnished urban Judaism. It reminds us of the resilience Jews needed to continue to observe their religious traditions in the city on its public streets. Being Jewish made one different from other, Christian Americans, and religious conflict on city streets sharpened a child's awareness of diversity even in a city and neighborhood where so many other Jews lived.

Although the impact of commerce on the streets of Jewish immigrant neighborhoods could be glimpsed in every major city where Jews settled, the Lower East Side grew into such a densely crowded area, with over seven hundred thousand Jewish residents at its peak, that it assumed an iconic character. It became the site where immigrant urban Judaism reached its most complex forms of expression. Often compared to Calcutta, the Lower East Side appeared to sweat humanity. It drew observers with cameras and pens, ready to picture in images and words what Judaism looked like on New York streets. And everything, or so it seemed, could be seen on those streets.[48]

Mothers nursed babies on the tenement stoops; children played games in the gutters. Boys and women carried bundles of cut but unsewn fabric through the streets, on their way to a tenement workshop. The steam of hot irons billowed from tenement windows, sure evidence of a sweatshop. People congregated and socialized, shopped and strolled. The street served as a kind of theater where one could observe everyday performances of urban Jewish life.

The immigrant Jewish Lower East Side engaged the senses: the raucous sounds of men and women in the market, shouting their wares; the roar of elevated trains overhead; the shrieks of children playing on the sidewalks; the clatter of sewing machines from open windows. The streets smelled from the stench of rotting food and horse excrement; the pungent odor of unwashed bodies crowded together in densely populated tenements without hot running water; the stale aroma of dank hallways seeped out onto the stoops; the sweet fragrance of baking bread wafted through the air. Tastes as well characterized the neighborhood: the flavors of roasted chickpeas purchased from carts, spicy pickles floating in barrels of brine, the fizzy pleasure of soda water, and the warmth of a glass of hot tea.

But more than anything the Lower East Side offered visual representations of Jews and Judaism as quintessentially urban, foreign, poor, and exotic. As the historian Beth Wenger observes, "Most American Jews have come to know the East Side through the widely reproduced photographs of Jacob Riis and Lewis Hine, through popular books such as Irving Howe's *World of Our Fathers*, or through the Hollywood images in 'Hester Street' and 'Crossing Delancey.'" These images retain their power to fascinate even after a century. Indeed a number of them have become heritage icons and a source of stories told about American Jews. However, "the development of nostalgia for immigrant life" involved "no retreat from the modernization and acculturation of Jews," but it was "an integral part of the ongoing reconstruction of Jewish consciousness in an American context."[49] Cities played a critical role in this process, none more than New York.

Visitors came down to the Lower East Side to watch life as it was lived for all to see. Some, like Protestant social reformer and "investigative-reporter-turned-photographer" Jacob Riis, toted enormous cameras to record the crowds, the dirt, and the incredible density of the Jewish districts that seemed to lack even room to breathe. The crowded streets, outdoor markets, red-light district, and innumerable children enticed both the curious and concerned. Their images have fixed in our mind's eye what a Jewish immigrant neighborhood looked like. A crusading photographer such as Riis dragged his bulky camera not only into the alleys and rookeries but also into dark tenement basements to show his middle-class audiences "how the other half lives."[50]

The Byron brothers also frequented immigrant streets at the turn of century. When their photographs of the marketplace did not match the press of flesh summoned by sharp-tongued observers writing in the popular papers, they were not above compositing a couple of images to make shopping on Hester Street match viewers' expectations.[51] Visitors with cameras invited residents to pose but also took pictures without permission, peering into kitchens and workshops, and onto fire escapes, those extra bedrooms for sleeping on hot summer nights. Above all, however, outdoor commerce attracted them. "Some observers of the urban landscape viewed pushcart markets as picturesque places steeped in urban cosmopolitanism."[52]

Lewis Hine's photograph *Market Day in the Jewish Quarter, 1905* exemplifies one form of what became a genre. Hine understood photography as a form of social work, partaking of the spirit of Progressive politics.[53] He took this photograph of Rivington Street looking east across Orchard Street from an elevated location in the middle of the block (probably from an elevated train station) looking down on the crowds. From this vantage point he managed to picture the scene unobserved.

Lewis W. Hine, *Market Day in the Jewish Quarter*, 1905. Courtesy Photography Collection, Miriam and Ira D. Wallach Division of Art, Prints and Photographs, New York Public Library, Astor, Lenox and Tilden Foundations.

Both men and women stroll on the sidewalk, but women appear to talk to women and men to men. Gendered norms of behavior govern these public spaces. Pushcarts line the gutter, offering food for sale. A woman in the foreground appears to be making a purchase from a young man wearing a cap as another man in a hat watches her. Farther back on the block a woman sits on a chair with her back to the street. She apparently is watching a storefront, perhaps to ensure that nothing is stolen. Signs in Yiddish for a kosher butcher and in English for a bakery hang from a second story. Wagons rumble down the center of the street. The scene is lively and stretches endlessly for blocks into the horizon.

On the right in between two tenement buildings stands the First Roumanian-American Congregation building. Synagogues wedged within the street façade speak to their integral participation in street life. Although the bustle of commerce attracted Hine's attention and portrayed Jewish immigrant life more powerfully than a synagogue building, his photograph conveys a sense that business overwhelmed religious life.[54] Only by thinking of the two as intimately intertwined is it possible to recognize how Judaism encompassed both street commerce and synagogue services.

On these busy streets both attending synagogue services on Friday evening and seeing a Yiddish show expressed ways of being Jewish in the urban world. "My father did go to *shul* regularly and I usually went with him," recalled the lyricist Yip Harburg, but ". . . the house of God never had much appeal for me." Harburg found "a substitute temple—the theater. Poor as we were, on many a Saturday, after services, my father packed me up and told my mother that we were going to *shul* to hear a *magid* [preacher]. But somehow, instead of getting to the *magid* from Slutsk we always arrived at the Thalia Theater where the great Madame Lipsik or Tomashevsky was performing."[55] Religious services competed with urban entertainments and often, as Harburg attests, lost out.

Children spent most of their time on the streets when not in school. By the age of ten most were deemed independent. Many joined popular social and athletic clubs (SACs). These informal associations drew together boys of roughly the same age who lived on the same blocks. Street games were largely segregated by gender; boys played together, as did girls. "On the street, you were judged by how you hit the ball, how you made out with the girls, how you stood up in a rhubarb, how much punishment you could take and how much you could dish out," Gus Tyler recalled. "In the process," the Jewish union leader concluded, "I learned that man does not live by words alone—even if he is Jewish."[56]

Arthur Leipzig, who like Tyler grew up in Brooklyn, pictured that reality. In 1943 while working on the newspaper PM, he shot his first major photo essay: *Children's Games*. "The streets were an extension of the home," he recalled. "They were the living rooms and the playgrounds, particularly for the poor whose crowded tenements left little room for play." Throughout working-class urban neighborhoods, "the children occupied the streets, now and then allowing a car or truck to pass." Inspired by a print of a "wonderful painting" by Peter Brueghel the Elder (1560) that depicted all sorts of children's pastimes in the sixteenth century, he started to photograph urban recreation on Brooklyn's streets. Leipzig "was struck by how similar games played nearly four hundred years earlier in Flanders were to the ones being played outside" his window. He eventually photographed dozens, from "Johnny on the Pony" to

Arthur Leipzig, *Chalk Games*, ca. 1943. © Arthur Leipzig. Courtesy Arthur Leipzig.

"Hide and Seek" to "Follow the Leader," seeking to document as many different activities as possible. His photo *Chalk Games* captures the intricacy of children's pursuits, their imagination, and the vital world of the street.[57]

Occasionally, these SACs blossomed into more formal organizations, as was the case with the Brownsville Boys Club. The club grew out of efforts by teenagers to petition the New York City Board of Education in 1940 to reopen after-school recreation facilities to boys over the age of fourteen. These boys, members of such clubs as the Chrislotts, the Stonedales, and the Newport Indians (names reflecting intersecting corners of the blocks where they lived), determined to do more than petition: they confederated and mobilized to secure space for athletic events. What these teenagers accomplished endured even after many grew up and left what they considered a "nurturing neighborhood."[58]

The streets of Jewish neighborhoods testified not only to recreation, consumption, religious holidays, and weekly Sabbaths but also to Jewish politics in its everyday clothes. Socialist political speakers regularly stood on soapboxes to preach their anticapitalist gospel and inspire their oppressed listeners to join the Socialist Party for their salvation. Zionist agitators also took to the streets to recruit supporters to help desperate Jews return to the land of Israel and thus usher in a messianic age when Jews would live in their own homeland, unafraid of persecution. Anarchists mocked them all. Any form of government would oppress and exploit. Jews needed to be free from the chains of religion and state.

These street-corner debates found sustenance in substantial buildings that announced their political leanings through their names. The Labor Lyceum in Brownsville, Brooklyn, considered "a shrine of the neighborhood," competed with Adath Israel, a hotbed of Zionist groups.[59] In Chicago the Hebrew Institute, "frankly Jewish and staunchly American," transformed into the Jewish People's Institute in 1922. It gained an enviable reputation when it relocated to the North Lawndale area in 1926 as a center of education, religion, recreation, and vocational training.[60] In the Boyle Heights section of Los Angeles Jews established a Jewish Community Center that reflected a strong commitment to intercultural education (a forerunner of today's multiculturalism). In 1949 they sponsored the Festival of Friendship, highlighting four different cultural groups in the area: African Americans, Mexicans, Japanese, and Jews. The festival culminated in a parade that drew fifteen hundred participants.[61] In short, in cities across the United States synagogues faced competition not only from street cultures but also from other proselytizing Jewish groups that proffered alternative ways to be Jewish in the urban milieu.

This competition even registered in response to one of the worst tragedies befalling American Jews, which occurred on Saturday, March 25, 1911, when a fire raged through the Triangle Shirtwaist Factory building in New York's Greenwich Village. The blaze trapped most of the young women working there because the Jewish owners of the factory had refused to sign with the International Ladies' Garment Workers' Union (ILGWU) when the women had gone out on strike in 1909. In addition, they also had locked the doors to the fire escapes, ignoring one of the safety measures championed by the union.

The building where the fire occurred that took the lives of 146 young women and men remained standing. (It is still standing; as part of New York University it houses classrooms and offices.) It was a fireproof building. Only the people inside the building burned to death. Although fire trucks raced to the scene, their ladders reached merely the sixth floor, but the eighth, ninth, and tenth floors were burning. With no way out except through the open windows, young women took their turn to stand on the window ledge, the flames licking their skirts, before stepping off and plummeting to the sidewalk below. A crowd of horrified bystanders helplessly watched the women fall to their deaths. Not until the World Trade Towers attack did New Yorkers see another such horror unfold in their midst.[62]

One of the most powerful public funeral marches also served as a protest march: it buried the unidentified remains of victims of the terrible Triangle Shirtwaist Factory fire. Both Orthodox Jews and socialist Jews laid claim to the Jewish victims, mostly teenaged girls. Since these two groups of Jews had sparred over who should lead the funeral march and where the victims should be buried, the *troyermarsh* or funeral march took place separately from the burial. Despite pouring rain 120,000 joined its ranks. The march united Jewish unionists from the Lower East Side with uptown non-Jewish unionists and members of the Women's Trade Union League. Catholics, Protestants, and Jews all participated in the public commemoration, but despite the predominant Jewish deaths hardly "a distinctly Jewish voice was heard."[63]

Although laboring on the Sabbath did not end with the deaths of so many young Jewish women, legislation to protect workers from fire did help to initiate a new awareness of the importance of safeguards. The committee established to investigate the fire discovered itself schooled in Progressive politics. Jewish socialists served as researchers and conveyed their insights and values to men, such as Al Smith and Robert Wagner, who would go on to important careers as New York State's governor and senator, respectively.

By World War I, the immigrant neighborhood's reputation as a colorful slum had been secured, just at the point when several decades' worth of outmigration had substantially decreased its population. "During the interwar years, the East Side ceased to be the center of Jewish population and activity," Wenger argues, "and became instead a primary site of Jewish memory and a physical space for the invention of Jewish identity in America." Because they no longer lived on the Lower East Side, New

York Jews could embellish its reputation as a distinctly Jewish American urban place. "The East Side provided a grounded, tangible space where American Jews fashioned their own image of the Jewish past," Wenger writes, something they could do from the vantage point of more prosperous urban neighborhoods. "Nostalgia for the immigrant neighborhood provided a geographic space where native-born Jews could trace their roots as Jewish Americans." At the same time, the Lower East Side "came to embody the many contradictions of second-generation Jewish life."[64]

Jews were leaving the Lower East Side for Brooklyn and the Bronx, as they were leaving immigrant areas in large cities across the United States. In fact Jews had started to leave as soon as rapid transit became available, in part because acres of tenements were leveled to build bridges and roadways. Lower East Side Jews were moving uptown to the West Side if they could afford it or across the river to Williamsburg and Brownsville if they were still struggling. While this outmigration dramatically reduced the density of the Jewish population on the Lower East Side, it neither changed its reputation nor altered the preponderance of immigrant Jews as the area's primary residents. Similarly Jews were departing the Near West Side of Chicago for Lawndale, a newer working-class and lower-middle-class neighborhood farther north and west. And in cities across the United States, Jews were moving to streetcar suburbs, to Roxbury and Dorchester in Boston, to Strawberry Mansion in Philadelphia, to Cleveland Heights.

Louis Wirth, a pioneering immigrant Jewish urban sociologist who studied Chicago's Jewish immigrant neighborhood, claimed, "Not until the immigrant leaves the ghetto does he become fully conscious of himself and his status. He feels a sense of personal freedom and expansion as he takes up his residence in the more modern and less Jewish area" of Lawndale. Wirth noted that Jews, initially barred from residence in this German and Irish section of town, quickly transformed it into a neighborhood of densely settled apartment houses. In Wirth's calculus, this new area became a second "ghetto" with a corresponding social and psychological profile. "If you would know what kind of a Jew a man is," he wrote, "ask him where he lives; for no single factor indicates as much about the character of the Jew as the area in which he lives. It is an index not only to his economic status, his occupation, his religion, but to his politics and his outlook on life and the stage in the assimilative process that he has reached." Wirth knit together Jewish urban geography into a powerful predictive tool. Look at people's addresses, and so many details about their lives would unfold.[65]

Wirth's insights relied on the distributive effects of class and ethnicity on urban migration. Jews, and other urban residents, did tend to move together to different sections of a city. Jewish real estate entrepreneurs and Jewish builders as well as accessibility of public transit and networks of friends and relatives guided Jews' collective choices. But anti-Semitic restrictive covenants also constrained them. The result often produced remarkably homogeneous neighborhoods, that is, neighborhoods where Jews of a similar class position made up around half of the total population rather than a majority. These sections of the city soon acquired their own street life—different from immigrant enclaves but nonetheless visibly Jewish. Judaism's requisites had not changed with greater economic security, but their expression took new urban forms.

As I have previously argued, "For Jews, the shift from immigrant enclave to ethnic neighborhood marked the transition into the urban landscape of modernity." Jews contributed to the physical forms of their urban world as well as their emerging spirit. In the city spaces they inhabited they integrated religious and cultural resources and social organizations and networks, with class and ideology and encoded these on the cityscape. In second-generation neighborhoods where the children of immigrants lived, streets exuded a kind of middle-class Jewish urbanism.[66] While the physical dimensions of these neighborhoods varied from art deco apartment buildings in the Bronx to private and two-family homes in Detroit, the apartment house became "the emblem of the Jews' love affair with the city."[67] Apartment houses produced relative density, in comparison with single- or two-family homes, and often accompanied the segregation of shopping to commercial streets. Professional suites for doctors and dentists usually occupied ground floors rather than stores.

The buildings that lined city streets helped to shape the religious culture that emerged on them. They provided more than a seamless backdrop for Jewish urban life. They became the new environment through which Jews lived their religion. Tenements, or multifamily dwellings without separate baths or elevators, housed the immigrant poor. Jews did their best to leave these overcrowded miserable residences. Flats, with separate baths in multifamily buildings with stairs ("walk-ups" as they were known), provided homes for the middle classes. Apartment houses, consisting of suites of rooms with private baths in elevator buildings, catered to the upper classes. "But in the 1920s, builders began designing apartment houses for the middle classes, enabling those living in walk-ups to rent apartments in elevator buildings." They adopted art deco architecture as an exuberant theatrical style that best expressed an urbane modernity to appeal to upwardly mobile immigrants and their children. Evidence of their enthusiasm endures along the streets around the Grand Concourse in the Bronx where Jewish builders and architects "covered many blocks with yellow brick, curving apartments that flaunted geometric motifs, recessed entrance ways with precast concrete panels, corner windows and roof lines with metal railings." Interior spaces sported "mosaic ceilings, tiled floors, incised elevator doors and metal reflecting radiator covers." Their lively public spaces of lobbies, hallways, elevators, rooftops, and stairways mediated between private Jewish living space and public American street space. But intermingling of Jewish and American also occurred on the streets. Children growing up in these apartments learned to decode the messages of the streets and reckoned their Jewishness "as part of the common coin of urban discourse."[68]

Performative possibilities for Jewish urban life appeared in these new urban areas. "If Jewish architects and builders set the stage—a stage they built for various New Yorkers, not just for Jews—Jewish residents produced the play. They chose to live in certain neighborhoods, and not in others."[69] They then created in these city spaces a pluralist Jewish milieu. The commerce and culture of the streets and the organizations located in the neighborhood endowed these urban areas with a Jewish aura. They became recognizably Jewish places. "Jews were Jews because of where they lived," observes Riv-Ellen Prell. "Jews lived their lives in urban streets, air, and public spaces. Even streets that catered to Jewish needs became a version of a Jewish civic square."[70] Although Yiddish signage diminished together with the spoken language, kosher food stores, bookstores, and religious organizations all found room in these burgeoning sections of the city. These largely residential neighborhoods with designated shopping streets nearby emanated urban rhythms that differed from immigrant sections. Children still played on the sidewalks and married women walked to do their grocery shopping. But men usually left the neighborhood to go to work, taking rapid transit to jobs located downtown.

One important characteristic of public expressions of Jewish religious life endured: on Jewish holidays, Jews filled the sidewalks wearing their finery. Only now they often promenaded along graceful, tree-lined streets. Certain large boulevards acquired a Jewish ambiance where elements of urban lived religion could be observed: the Grand Concourse in the Bronx, Eastern Parkway in Brooklyn, the Boardwalk in Atlantic City, Collins Avenue in Miami. Some Jews went to synagogue, of course, but others just took the opportunity of a day at leisure to walk with family and meet friends and neighbors. Prell calls this urban milieu "a spatial Judaism."[71]

The writer Vivian Gornick thought that "organic quality of the atmosphere" in her East Bronx neighborhood "told us who we were, gave us boundary and idiomatic reference, shaped the face of the culture in which each of us assumed a vital, albeit primitive, sense of identity."[72] Neighborhood boundaries, invisible to all but the initiated, conferred status on urban Jews. As Prell points out, "It was about being in a place rather than participating in any particular facet of it."[73] On Passover and Yom Kippur, Gornick writes, "we did not have to be 'observing' Jews to know that we were Jews." The urban neighborhood gave this gift of a distinctive religious identity to all its Jewish residents. Gornick, a nonobserving Jew, remembered that "the whole world shut down, everyone dressed immaculately, and a sense of awe thickened the very air we breathed."[74]

Of course not all memoirs of growing up Jewish in the city celebrated this bequest of urban Judaism. Jazz critic and journalist Nat Hentoff's memoir, *Boston Boy*, vividly describes his rebellious rejection of Jewish piety. He grew up in the Jewish neighborhood of Dorchester and Roxbury, an area with forty synagogues (all but two Orthodox) and dozens of kosher butcher shops and bakeries, not to mention the G&G deli on Blue Hill Avenue. Hentoff recalls sitting on the porch of his house in the heart of the neighborhood, scoffing at his more observant neighbors by eating a salami sandwich as they walked to synagogue services on the fast day of Yom Kippur. Such a personal denial of Judaism required an audience, one provided by the city's streets. This Jewish milieu both sustained Judaism and allowed disobedient sons and daughters to express themselves. Indeed Hentoff considers his "life as a heretic" a tradition he keeps "precisely because I am a Jew." Urban neighborhoods sustained this Jewish "tradition" as well.[75]

By contrast in the Orthodox Jewish neighborhood of Borough Park in Brooklyn, with its tree-lined streets and urban ambience, many of the prominent synagogues "required their officers and clergy to wear formal dress on Sabbaths and holidays."[76] Thus on these days men wearing elegant clothes and top hats could be seen strolling the area's sidewalks.

These balmy days of prosperity fell victim to the Great Depression; then political conflict again rocked the streets. When Jewish landlords refused to reduce rents, Jewish tenants went on strike. After landlords obtained eviction notices and city marshals came to enforce them, neighbors rallied to fight the evictions. In a section of the Bronx where many socialist and communist Jews lived, these demonstrations occasionally turned violent. But success in opposing evictions happened "precisely because Jews not ideologically committed to radical causes proved willing to participate. When a group of tenants initiated a rent strike, hundreds and sometimes thousands of Jewish neighbors rallied to their defense." Wenger concludes that as tenant strikes and protests swept through working-class districts of the city, women played crucial roles as activists. "The women are the fighters, the pickets, the agitators," wrote the *Jewish Daily Forward*. "A remarkable bravery and battle-cheer is displayed by the women in the rent strikes." Women stood at the heart of these neighborhood battles, unafraid of using the streets to advance the justice of their cause. They relied on their neighbors to help with unattended chores and to watch their children.[77]

Lessons learned during the Great Depression picketing in front of tenements translated into tactics after World War II when Jews in cities throughout the United States rallied in support of Zionist efforts to establish a Jewish state. Although Britain only recently had been the staunch ally of the United States in the fight against Nazism and Fascism, Jews vigorously protested British policies on Palestine that restricted Jewish immigration from European displaced persons camps where Jewish survivors of the Holocaust were confined. Wherever a British consulate existed—from Miami to Philadelphia to Chicago to Los Angeles—Jews joined picket lines with signs comparing British behavior in 1946 to their actions in 1776. In a bid for Irish American support, some added "Ireland 1922" as a reminder of British perfidy.[78]

The integration of the state of Israel after its establishment in 1948 into American Jews' urban Judaism did not develop until the 1960s when May Day parades, which had attracted substantial contingents of Jewish communists, had largely disappeared. In 1964 a largely impromptu parade in New York City down Riverside Drive along the West Side of Manhattan spurred organization of a regularly scheduled Salute to Israel. Parades featuring ethnic groups, from Italians on Columbus Day to the Irish on St. Patrick's Day, attracted political attention even as they blurred distinctions between religion and ethnicity. A parade celebrating Israel achieved similar goals. In its earliest formation it united secular Zionists with more religiously observant Jews in a common expression of urban Judaism. After extensive migration to the suburbs, Israel parades in various cities increasingly drew on suburban Jews, who traveled into town to watch their children march.

In the years after World War II, some New York Jews transported their ways of living Judaism to new cities. There they began a process of transforming Judaism into an urban leisure-time public activity. Many traveled to Miami Beach, first to vacation and later to linger as "snowbirds." The Jewish population boomed after World War II when Jews discovered the city, guided there in part by Jewish hotel entrepreneurs. Soon Jews were not just visiting the city but "getting sand in their feet." They decided to stay, especially those who were able to retire on Social Security and their union pensions. So Miami Beach acquired an elderly Jewish population un-self-conscious about their Jewish behavior. Leisure living invited expressive forms of Jewish religious observance. Folk singing in Collins Park, Israeli dancing at the band shell by the beach, Yiddish conversations on benches and chairs set beside the sidewalk all spoke to forms of Jewish lived religion. Of course kosher eateries—restaurants, delis, and cafeterias—followed Jews.

By the 1980s as this way of life was disappearing, a number of photographers visited Miami Beach to picture what seemed to be both exotic and incongruous. Elderly Jews dancing, singing, strolling, sitting amid palm trees and sandy beaches struck an odd chord in the eyes of younger Jews unaccustomed to such public postures. Here was an unusual version of living Judaism, somewhat hedonistic and oriented toward leisure yet seemingly intimate rather than boasting an anonymity associated by suburbanites with a bustling fast-paced resort city. At least that was the attitude of the photographer Richard Nagler, who thought he saw the last idealized remnants of European shtetl Jews on Miami Beach in the 1980s. The Yiddish writer I. B. Singer, who might have known better, did not discourage him but penned a brief introduction to Nagler's photo book, *My Love Affair with Miami Beach*, as his own love letter to this improbable island city.

Nagler's photograph of the practice of *tashlich*, where Jews symbolically cast their sins of the past year into a flowing body of water during the holy day of Rosh Hashanah, captures some of those complicated emotions. Nagler pictures Jews not in prayer but with their backs to

Richard Nagler, *Beach Scene—Rosh Hashanah, September 1986*.
© Richard Nagler. Courtesy Richard Nagler.

the camera, walking away from the ocean's edge. They are dressed not for the beach but in formal clothes appropriate for the synagogue—a suit or jacket and slacks, hat or cap. The men carry prayer books. In front of them graffiti on the beach patrol headquarters announces "Sojo Cristo"—a reminder of the religiously plural society in which Jews live. On Miami Beach and in other big cities throughout the United States where large numbers of Jews resided comfortably, they always lived among Christians, both Protestants and Catholics. Yet consciousness of their minority status did not inhibit Jews from public expressions of Judaism.

Jews moved out of cities to the suburbs for many reasons. Sometimes they pursued what was promoted by federal mortgage and highway policies as "the American dream"; other times fear of African Americans as neighbors spurred them to move. Aspirations to own a house, with its promise of more space and privacy, also propelled Jews to leave cities, as did desires for personal security and upward mobility. Usually a confluence of these forces set them moving. Yet they did not lose their connections with urban space. In addition to traveling downtown for work, many Jews began to craft versions of urbanism that somehow allowed them to participate in its spirit even from afar.[79]

These interpretations often encouraged understanding cities and their old immigrant neighborhoods less as living remnants than as heritage sites where American Judaism took root. Just as visiting the Touro Synagogue in Newport, Rhode Island, moved Emma Lazarus, so did a similar visit to a crumbling monument of Moorish architecture, the Eldridge Street Synagogue, inspire Roberta Brandes Gratz. Gratz helped to restore the building and convert it into a museum. She saw her project "less in terms of its relevance to the cultural life of the New York Jewish community than in terms of Jewish acceptance and presence in the wider context of American society and national heritage," argues the anthropologist Jack Kugelmass. "Eldridge Street is an important vessel the same way that Trinity Church, North Church in Boston, or any of the other important churches that we think of as significant markers of American history," she affirmed. Ignoring the Newport synagogue, she continued, "we've never put a synagogue in that galaxy." From her perspective, Eldridge Street Synagogue claimed for American Jews "its rightful place in the thread of American history that is so ethnically based." Her conflation of ethnicity and religion—Boston's North Church and Trinity Church more often stand for Protestant Christianity than they represent white Anglo ethnicity—reveals the extent to which urban Judaism appeared to American Jews to express an ethnic Jewish immigrant identity. Gratz's activities fit with her larger theories of urbanism, her commitment to local, small-scale efforts to recycle buildings to preserve neighborhood complexity as opposed to massive renewal projects.[80]

Her efforts, starting in the early 1980s, coincided with a burst of tourism to the Lower East Side by American Jews who interpreted a visit to the urban neighborhood "as akin to going 'home'—a home unseen for many years and clouded with nostalgia." This "home" often as not bore little relationship to the experience of immigrant ancestors, but the Lower East Side became an icon of the American Jewish past, "a deliberate, willed act of creation."[81] As Seth Kamil notes, "Tourism itself has helped to maintain the vitality of the Jewish neighborhood."[82] Walking the streets, something impossible to do in suburban subdivisions, enticed Jews eager to reclaim a piece of a dimly remembered—and often rejected—past. Cities had figured in that past, and now some desired to savor the urban experience, even if only for a few hours. Significantly one of Kamil's very first tours of the Jewish Lower East Side occurred on Christmas Day in 1991. He explicitly targeted Jews seeking an alternative to Christian holiday celebrations.[83]

But nothing illustrates the impulse to transform urban Judaism into American heritage better than the Lower East Side Tenement Museum, established in 1988. Ruth Abram grew up in the segregated South and chafed at the racial restrictions separating her as a white person from African Americans and the social exclusions separating her as a Jew from Christians. Her childhood world was located a considerable distance from Boyle Heights and its multicultural Festival of Friendship. After she moved to New York, she discovered the power of the ordinary tenement building at 97 Orchard Street on the Lower East Side to promote her vision of interreligious and interracial toleration. Following months of futile searches for an empty building she had given up and decided to rent a storefront. When her confederate went to see the space she asked, "But where are the toilets?" So the landlord took her into the hallway in its miserable condition. Standing in the decrepit, dimly lit tenement hall whose silent walls bore witness to the difficult lives of so many immigrants to the United States, Abram experienced an epiphany like Emma Lazarus at the Touro Synagogue. At that moment "she felt she was standing on hallowed ground," Abram recounted. The Tenement Museum possessed a redemptive mission. It would preserve the experiences and cultural memories of people long ignored.[84]

According to Abram,

> The tenement building represented the common ground of immigrants from everywhere. Through it, one could discuss the history of immigration and immigrant life, the role of reformers, of government, the history of housing and our changing views as to what was an acceptable life style. But most all, through a tenement museum, the general public, old and young alike could be invited to consider this question: How will we be one nation and at the same time enjoy, appreciate and certainly not be afraid of the profound differences we bring to the table based on background.

Abram sought, in short, to answer the question of the Fourth of July parade with its separate tables of kosher food.[85]

In seeking common ground, the Tenement Museum focused on problems of poverty, family pathologies (husbands' abandonment of their wives and children), and interreligious interdependence (an Italian girl's experiences of being a *shabbes goy* and turning on the lights for Orthodox Jews on the Sabbath). Yet Jews coming to visit either the Tenement Museum or the museum at Eldridge Street tended to imagine that the whole neighborhood somehow was sacred. The streets themselves, not just the synagogues or the tenements, possessed heroic, mythic dimensions. They produced those formative experiences in the lives of Jewish immigrants that in turn led to the emergence of American Judaism.

Kugelmass suggests that the Lower East Side constitutes a "site of memory whose architectural, graphic, and olfactory sensuality stands so much at odds with the aesthetic, social and historical flatness of the suburban landscapes that have long been the locus of American Jewish life."[86] Given the physical and social and economic mobility of American Jews, they needed an enduring site of origin. What better place of origin than an urban immigrant neighborhood? The Lower East Side, long visited, photographed, described, and deplored, had escaped gentrification in the 1980s yet retained Jewish stores and a small Jewish population, ironically secured, unlike the populations of other immigrant areas, by affordable apartment houses sponsored by the ILGWU and the Amalgamated Clothing Workers Union produced by leveling tenements. Accessible and located in New York City, which remained the source of Jewish American culture for much of the century, and a touchstone of authentic Jewishness even for those living thousands of miles west of the Hudson River, the Lower East Side embodies the urban origins of American Judaism. It does so in part because it "stands almost as a point of mediation between the labor-based politics of the American Jewish past" and its current political stances. "For Jews struggling with the huge distance that now exists between their social standing and their politics, the Lower East Side is a concrete reminder of a time when their language, politics, and even kinship networks were intricately connected to an organic community," Kugelmass concludes.[87]

Jewishness came naturally on the streets; there was no need to do anything special. These dimensions to Jewish religious observance, or what can also be called lived religion that does not discriminate between custom and commandment (*minhag* and *mitzvah*), gradually disappeared in suburbs where Jews lived next door to non-Jews and car culture replaced street culture. Leaving behind city streets, irrespective of whether those streets were in working-class or middle-class areas, Jews lost many of the public faces o&f Jdaism, seen in commerce, on signs, in interactions with others, in speech and gestures, even in politics. While Conservative Judaism attempts to include aspects of urban Judaism within synagogue centers, institutional constraints often prevent synagogues from expanding. Similarly Chabad's energetic promotion of public displays of Hanukkah menorahs, usually located in city centers, only nods toward an urban Judaism. But just as heritage entrepreneurs returned to cities to reclaim and reimagine Judaism's urban origins through tourism and museums, so have artists and photographers evoked these worlds, inviting Jews to enter Jewish streets of the past through memoir, fiction, poetry, and film.

CHAPTER 3

SNAPSHOTS

In 1966 Allon Schoener curated a powerful and wildly popular exhibit at the Jewish Museum in New York City—the exhibit was so popular, in fact, that officials extended it for several months, an unprecedented decision. *The Lower East Side: Portal to American Life* chronicled the world of immigrant Jews in part through snapshots drawn from newspapers.[1] Schoener dramatically enlarged a number of these photos so that they covered entire walls, immersing viewers in the city streets. These innovative "photomurals" as they would subsequently be called aimed to re-create Jewish urban space within the museum's precincts. The exhibit marked a new venture for the Jewish Museum. The first in "a series of interpretive historical exhibitions that compelled American Jews at the grass roots to take a hard and searching look at their own history," the exhibit "enlarged the museum's capacity for emotional engagement even as [it] deepened its role as a sophisticated purveyor of ideas." Historian Jenna Weissman Joselit argues for the "newfound relevance of historical exhibitions to the Jewish civic imagination." Grandparents corralled their grandchildren to see the show, producing long lines outside the museum. Schoener included drawings and paintings by Jewish artists as well as Yiddish theater posters, playbills, song sheets, and even simulated sounds of peddlers. His theatrical flair transformed museum practice and, more important for American Jews, brought photographs into a conjoined realm of art and history where they opened a window into the Jewish urban past. Photographs gave Jews a path backward into the urban origins of American Judaism. As Joselit observes, the exhibit "redefined the notion of history, claiming it as a visual medium, not just a textual one."[2]

This chapter examines selected images that came to represent urban Judaism to American Jews. It argues that these snapshots of the past translated urban Judaism not only into the history of American Jews but also into a meaningful aspect of their lives. Viewed from suburban split-levels or even comfortable apartments, photographs connected Jews across generations and helped them interpret and understand themselves. Placed next to family pictures, photos of the urban world prior to World War II anchored both experiences and memories of those who viewed them. Many of these photographs actually lived multiple lives, first when they were originally taken and published, and then when they were reprinted in other contexts. Their own stories and the subsequent stories each photo seemed to tell made tangible an evanescent past. Gradually, as the immigrant era faded from memory, Jews came to narrate crucial dimensions of their history through these visual images.

Both Christian and Jewish observers pictured the city. Although they often held different views on what they saw, the photos themselves were interpreted as compelling narratives of Jewish engagement with the urban world. Relatively few Jews could actually get to visit the Lower East Side, but far more could enjoy pictures of their "Plymouth Rock," or, as Schoener called it, their "portal to America." As many Jews became documentary photographers in the twentieth century, they sought to establish a genealogy for their type of photographic practice. Thus they reclaimed old photographs from the turn of the century and gave them a new life and audience. Together these dual influences produced growing recognition of the power of photography to capture liminal moments in time and space. Snapshots froze complex transitions from Old World to New, from immigrant slum to streetcar suburb, preserving a visual record of ordinary urban behaviors.

Popular photography and mass immigration arrived in American cities at roughly the same time at the turn of the last century. Art historian Rebecca Zurier observes that the "trend toward a pictorial city was economic." Specifically she argues that the advent of national corporations "encouraged the large-scale mass production and commercial promotion of images. . . . Partly to appeal to a new public of non-English-speaking or illiterate consumers who now wielded discretionary income, advertising at this time began to rely upon pictures rather than text."[3] This coincidence, along with technological changes that facilitated reproduction of photographs, also encouraged identification of Jews as immigrants. In addition interest in both the camera's potential for social work, that is, to promote social reform, and political uses of photography provided an impetus for enduring portraits of immigrant Jews.

Most images of immigrant Jews in these years were produced not by fellow Jews but by sympathetic or curious observers drawn to the densely crowded Jewish Lower East Side of New York City either as an exotic site or as a deplorable slum. As has been noted, outsiders with reform agendas such as Lewis Hine and Jacob Riis used photographs of Jewish immigrants to advance their causes. Riis wanted middle-class New Yorkers to support decent housing for the poor; Hine sought to motivate politicians to enact legislation restricting child labor. In the process they helped to launch a documentary tradition of photography. They also left behind the first enduring images of American Jews. In their photographs as well as the numerous street scenes of pushcart markets, American Jews learned to see themselves through the eyes of others.[4] Indeed scholar Sara Blair argues for the embeddedness of "photography itself in a specific site in which both Jewishness and modernity were being made and remade, tested and contested: the real and symbolic, variably iconic Lower East Side."[5] In fact the rediscovery of Jacob Riis by the Jewish photographer Alexander Alland and the championing of Lewis Hine by the largely Jewish New York Photo League in the 1930s and 1940s gave their work new audiences among American Jews and Jewish American photographers after World War II.[6]

Because of their narrative qualities, these snapshots of an urban world prodded American Jews to produce accounts that would become part of American Judaism's distinctive history. The Jewish immigrant neighborhood viewed through its photographs gradually changed from what scholar Pierre Nora calls a "site of history" into "a site of memory"—that is, it acquired symbolic, material, and functional dimensions. The city's social spaces exerted a collective impact on Jews, especially once they had left the city, influencing what could be and was remembered. Photographs—snapshots of the past—encoded Jewish urban memory. But as Nora points out, "There must be a will to remember." Each memory site exists to stop time, "to block the work of forgetting, . . . to materialize the immaterial," and yet each memory site exists only because of its "capacity for metamorphosis."[7]

The process started with Jacob Riis in the 1880s when he began lugging his huge, awkward cameras and tripods, along with dangerous magnesium flash pans, into New York's darkened tenements. A Christian immigrant from Denmark, Riis followed the police on their rounds to uncover the pathologies of the poor and to demonstrate the virtues of the vicious.[8] He wanted to change attitudes toward "the other half" to convince skeptical observers of his lantern shows of the fundamental humanity of poverty-stricken immigrants and of their right to decent living conditions.[9] He soon discovered that his photographs proved more effective than his words. In his autobiography he remarked that his writing "did not make much of an impression—these things rarely do, put in mere words—until my negatives, still dripping from the dark-room, came to reinforce them. From them there is no appeal."[10] They provided irrefutable evidence. Viewers could not turn away from them. Riis's dramatic language endowed his forays into the slums with elements of heroism. "His pictures," American studies scholar Alan Trachtenberg notes, "were taken as sensational disclosures of hidden social facts."[11]

The rise of printing processes to reproduce photographs in popular magazines and newspapers coincided with a new fascination with urban life. New York City at the turn of the twentieth century became "the image capital," as Zurier calls it—the center of the nation's fashion, publishing, advertising, and entertainment industries.[12] But photography's power to shock and educate, to entertain and enlighten led to images of Jews as impoverished and strange newcomers to the United States, living in foreign and overcrowded sections of the city.

Two photographs by Jacob Riis in particular shape our understanding of American Jewish immigrant life and the urban origins of American Judaism. Both images were captured indoors, in cramped and unpleasant quarters. Both portray elements of Jewish tradition that have been distorted by urban poverty. Both show men and boys, identifying Jewish religious practice with male Jews. In one case Riis captures a religious school study session in which Hebrew language and sacred text are supposedly transmitted from one generation to the next. In the other Riis photographs a man on a Friday evening, getting ready to observe and bless the Sabbath, a day of rest. Both photographs offer little hope for the redemptive possibilities of either text study or ritual practice. Even as he pictures efforts to reconstitute Jewish life in America, Riis reveals impossible difficulties confronting immigrants.

In *Talmud School in Hester Street Tenement*, taken around 1890, Riis conveys the oppressive conditions Jewish boys suffered in their or their parents' quest for learning. There is nothing here to suggest spiritual pursuits, not even a book. The boys sit on uncomfortable wooden benches, some with a shelf to hold books. They wear knee pants, a sign of their youth, and heavy coats, an indication of the cold weather outdoors and lack of warmth indoors. Most are too young for their feet to reach the floor. They sit quietly and stare at the photographer. In the background can be seen the *melamed*, the teacher, holding a very young child. On the

Jacob Riis, *Talmud School in Hester Street Tenement*, ca. 1890. Courtesy Museum of the City of New York.

wall hang cloaks and sacks. A large potbelly stove occupies the foreground. Riis is as interested in the potbelly stove, the peeling walls, the old-fashioned benches, and the meager light from the gas lamp in the squalid room as he is in the boys themselves. Their curious expressions come from the flash and heavy camera apparatus. Riis's photograph reminds middle-class viewers of the inadequate circumstances under which the young scholars labor. His writing merely repeats what the image proclaims so loudly, except that he recognizes that "the schoolmaster is not rarely a man of some attainments who has been stranded there."[13]

Jewish viewers of the photograph, while they would have deplored the miserable surroundings pictured, undoubtedly recognized an image of a *heder*, the one-room school transplanted from Europe to urban America. Thus despite the evident poverty and absence of any texts, the scene would have reminded them of the far-from-ideal situation for learning in Eastern Europe and presented an admirable effort to transmit folkways and collective memories. In short, for Jews the image portrayed a powerful commitment to continuity of tradition even under disorienting conditions in the New World.

Similarly Riis's moving photo *Ludlow Street Hebrew Making Ready for Sabbath Eve in His Coal Cellar*, captured in 1895, invites the stares of New Yorkers who would never dare to enter such a dark and dangerous space. How can a person presume to live in such an environment, let alone to sanctify the Sabbath there? Riis conveys here piety, symbolized by the fresh challah, the plain oilcloth, the saltshaker, and the worn prayer book (*siddur*), but also misery amid such filthy surroundings. This is no place to live. Above the man's head can be seen a hat, and beside that a jacket hangs on a hook. Off to the right a man holds a shovel, a reminder that the image depicts a coal cellar. On the left a Yiddish signboard leans against the shelves advertising the "Hebrew's" occupation as a cobbler, albeit one without a permanent shop. The immigrant Jew is bearded, his pants threadbare at the knees. He looks forward, averting his gaze from the camera but accommodating the photographer's intrusiveness. Despite Riis's genuine desire to promote change in New York City's housing conditions, his photographs also invite a vision of slums as picturesque. "We continue to be thrilled by the exotic spectacle of the

Jacob Riis, *Ludlow Street Hebrew Making Ready for Sabbath Eve in His Coal Cellar*, 1895. Courtesy Museum of the City of New York.

slums," argues one critic with a touch of hyperbole.[14] Although Jews no longer inhabit urban slums in the United States, we may ask whether the appeal of Jews as exotic "others" remains part of the visual inheritance bequeathed by Riis's photographs.

Riis published the photograph for the first time on page 6 of a special Christmas edition of the *Journal* as part of a photo essay titled *Where Santa Will Not Go*. The title given the photograph in this context, *Where the Sound of Church Bells Never Goes*, with the additional comment "especially for the Journal," suggests that Riis was inviting viewers to understand the Jew's visible misery as a reflection of his "fallen" status and not just his poverty. Clearly not a Christian, he could not hear the saving sound of church bells with their message of the birth of Jesus Christ. Unlike the other people photographed for this special Christmas edition, who "were denied the visit of Santa because of poverty or immoral behavior," the Jewish cobbler suffered because of his religious identity.[15]

Yet when American Jews see this photograph in the twenty-first century, they imagine a heroic story of Jewish religious persistence, not to mention an affirmation that their own current "riches" originated in very acceptable "rags." Despite enduring unrelenting poverty Jews held on to their distinctive beliefs and practices, continuing to observe the Sabbath even under terrible physical conditions. Riis's photograph reproduced with the title *Ludlow Street Hebrew Making Ready for Sabbath Eve in His Coal Cellar* evokes forms of Jewish spiritual resilience more often associated with European Jews, and especially the photographs of Roman Vishniac, shot in Eastern Europe on the eve of World War II. Its identification as taken on Ludlow Street on the Lower East Side suggests to American Jews that Jewish spirituality successfully made the transition from Old World to New, endowing American Judaism with inspiring urban religious origins.

Yet as Blair reminds us, Riis's images "were rescued from photographic oblivion" in the aftermath of World War II by Alexander Alland, himself a Jewish immigrant who arrived in New York in 1923. Alland decided to track down, reprint, and publish the photographs that constituted Riis's journey into "how the other half lives." Alland's efforts resulted in an exhibit, *The Battle with the Slum, 1887–1897*, at the Museum of the City of New York in 1947. Alland's skill in photographic printing transformed Riis's workaday pictures and "made it possible for Riis's images to enter the photographic canon as such." Ironically, Blair points out, "both literally and symbolically, then, Riis was redeemed from photographic oblivion by legatees of the very 'Jewtown' whose culture and cityscape provoked his most vexed responses." ("Jewtown" was the name Riis gave to the Jewish Lower East Side.) As part of a generation of Jewish photographers coming of age in the 1930s, Alland participated in efforts to find models for a type of documentary practice that addressed the urban dimensions of Jewish life, especially on the Lower East Side.[16] When other Jewish photographers came to photograph Jewish life there, they too addressed a number of similar themes evident in Riis's pictures.

Arnold Eagle, born in Hungary in 1910, immigrated at the age of nineteen with his family to Brooklyn in 1929 and bought his first camera three years later. Working as a photo retoucher at a studio on the Lower East Side, he immediately started to photograph the poverty-stricken Jewish world around him, adopting a documentary style that incorporated elements of Riis's work. Eagle was fortunate because the WPA hired him in 1935 to photograph the neighborhood as well as the notorious area around and under the Second Avenue elevated, home to prostitutes, gangs, pawnshops, and bums. Eagle joined the New York Photo League in 1937, eager to share in its radical collaborative urban documentary projects.[17] The league attracted mostly young left-wing Jewish photographers who believed that "an honest viewpoint, a clean lens" possessed the power to transform society.[18] An FBI report of 1942 put it differently: "For the most part, the members are interested in the serious aspects of photography—that is documentary pictures of social significance. They are all pretty definitely pro-labor and a great many are obviously Communist in their leanings."[19] Eagle first worked on a collaborative project photographing the Jewish community of Brownsville, Brooklyn. But when he received a Federal Arts Project commission to photograph the Orthodox community of the Lower East Side in 1938, he embarked on a task that he anticipated might document the ways of life of a disappearing group of Jews.[20] Much like the photographer Roman Vishniac at the same time in Poland, Eagle portrayed with dignity holy and mundane days, as well as Jewish institutions of learning and caring.[21]

Eagle's photograph *The Yeshiva* suggests how much had changed in New York City in forty-five years. Riis would have approved of the large windows and modern desks. But Eagle had a different agenda; he was interested not in reform but in documenting a way of life that seems out of place in America despite the students' well-scrubbed appearance. The photograph shows a study room suffused with an almost holy light that illuminates the faces of the students and their texts. One can make out brick walls and fire escapes behind the large windows. The contrast with Riis's Hester Street Talmud Torah is obvious. This is not a tenement room. No stove dominates the image, implying that steam heat keeps the students warm. Eagle's picture presents serious students, grouped according to age, concentrating on their studies, sitting in neat rows on benches, and focusing on their sacred books. Only one boy, in the middle near the window, grins as he dutifully looks down, suggesting that the students cooperated with Eagle, just as they had done for Riis. On closer examination one realizes that not everyone has a desk; some make do with stacks of account books. But all are clean and neatly dressed; some

Arnold Eagle, *The Yeshiva*, ca. 1938. © Arnold Eagle. Courtesy Estate of Arnold Eagle.

cover their heads with caps, and others wear yarmulkes. They all ignore the photographer, a convention that reflected changing expectations as well as far more familiarity with photography by the 1930s.

Twenty years later, after the murder of millions of European Jews and the escape of small numbers of Hasidim and their Rebbes to the United States, Orthodox Jews regained some of the exoticism they had had in the days of Riis. Only now Jewish photographers viewed the act of transmitting tradition not as a pious though hopeless gesture but as a timeless and enduring practice. They saw beauty in something alien to American culture. Cornell Capa's photograph *Hebrew Lesson, Brooklyn, New York, 1955* carries us a considerable distance from Eagle's image of robust American yeshiva students in the 1930s. Through Capa's eyes these Jews appear as living relics of another, more pure age. The melamed leans over three young boys, several years younger than those in Riis's photograph. The teacher is in shadow, so all we see is his profile and a tender jaw and

Cornell Capa, *Hebrew Lesson, Brooklyn, New York*, 1955. © Magnum Photos.

neck. A sensuous play of light illuminates his skin. His large hat rises up beyond the picture frame; we can make out, too, wispy hairs of his short, untrimmed beard. But his two long curling *peos* (sidelocks) dangling down dominate the photograph. They identify him as a *Hasid*, a pious Jew (often called ultra-Orthodox) and follower of a Rebbe. One hand reaches down to guide a boy reading, and we follow it from the teacher's face to the printed page. As in Eagle's photo, Capa shows us the texts with their Hebrew letters. The boys cooperate with the photographer and ignore him, continuing with their studies.

The title tells us that they are in New York City, but the image does not evoke fast-paced urbanity. Rather students and teacher dwell in a timeless world, touched by neither poverty nor modernity. Even the wall reveals nothing of place or space; its mottled gray surface serves as foil for the subtle lighting that illuminates each child's encounter with sacred text. Here is a Judaism seemingly untouched by modernity's disasters. Yet the date invites us to recall those horrors. Furthermore, the title's date and place suggest that traditional Judaism has been recuperated and restored in what many consider America's most cosmopolitan city, albeit in the borough of Brooklyn. Urban Judaism has acquired new signifiers: Hasidic Jews.

Did Cornell Capa, a Jewish photographer born in Hungary like Eagle, see any relationship between himself and the man and boys whom he photographs? Hungary was a center of a vibrant Hasidism prior to the Holocaust, but Capa came from modernizing segments of the Jewish community. Born Cornell Friedmann in 1918, he moved to Paris in 1936 to join his older brother, the photographer Robert Capa, and study medicine. Cornell adopted his brother's new surname, began to make prints for him, and then decided to become a photojournalist like Robert. Cornell arrived in New York City in 1937; subsequently he served in the U.S. Army. Following the war he worked for *Life* magazine but left it after his brother's untimely death in Vietnam in 1954 to take up his responsibilities at Magnum, the photography cooperative that provided pictures to international publications.[22] Cornell Capa photographed Jews in the new state of Israel but did not focus on American Jews, who seemed far less newsworthy in those years.

Titling his picture of young boys at study "Hebrew Lesson" recalls earlier male Jewish traditions of study. The boys are learning to read basic texts. The photograph partakes of everyday experience, although it is far from most American Jews' understanding of the mundane. It would take them some time to learn to recognize themselves in such images. Then when they did perceive a connection, it was often by imagining how they, assimilated American Jews, appeared in the eyes of Christian Americans.[23] But by the end of the century, certainly after Barbra Streisand donned *streimel* and *kapote*, the large black fur-trimmed hat and silk gabardine coat of Hasidic Jews, to play a cross-dressing yeshiva student in the movie version of Isaac Bashevis Singer's *Yentl*, many immediately imagined Hasidim as related to American Jews. Distant cousins perhaps, but part of a continuum.[24]

Arnold Eagle's photograph *A Seder in America* from the 1940s differs radically from Riis's Sabbath in a Ludlow Street coal cellar. Eagle shares the impulse to portray Jewish religious practices with Riis, and he similarly emphasizes food but chooses to show an American family reminiscent of Norman Rockwell's popular wartime covers for the *Saturday Evening Post*.

Rockwell's *Freedom from Want* painting, which depicts a family gathered for Thanksgiving dinner, borrows from the same well of wholesomeness and wholeness. Around a table are faces of children and adults; at the center stands an elderly couple. The gray-haired grandmother is placing a huge turkey on an oval platter on the table before her admiring husband. Behind them light flows through white lace curtains. Before them the white tablecloth, glasses, and sparkling white dishes exude plenty.

A similar sense of order, abundance, and familial cohesion permeates Eagle's Passover photograph of an intergenerational gathering of Jewish parents and children, a vivid contrast with the poverty of the coal cellar. In the foreground a woman holds a bowl for the family patriarch. On the table are glass dishes, a decanter full of wine, a platter of matzah, two glass candlesticks, and a plate of eggs. Around the table gather three young children on the left and three young adults on the right. Less visible is an older woman on the right. All watch intently as the patriarch, leaning back on the customary pillow, performs the ritual washing of hands. The viewer's eye is drawn to the young man wearing glasses and a large skullcap, sitting on a settee. Behind him is a bay win-

Arnold Eagle, *A Seder in America*, ca. 1940s. © Arnold Eagle. Courtesy Estate of Arnold Eagle.

dow with plants. Lace curtains obscure our view beyond the house, but a tall Japanese-style vase perched on a radiator is visible on the left. Here is an American Judaism that is utterly wholesome and healthy. Here is a Jewish home that appears comfortable and recognizably American, including both lace curtains and Oriental knickknacks, not a single man alone in his miserable coal cellar but a complete family, with a woman, attired in lace collar and apron, performing the required roles of wife and mother. In Eagle's snapshot a Jewish religious ritual, washing hands from a bowl at the beginning of the festive Passover meal called a seder, has become almost as American as apple pie. Rather than frozen in time, as in Capa's photo of the boys studying under the tutelage of the Hasid, Eagle's portrait of a Jewish family dining in their parlor on this special Passover holiday portrays what Nora would consider a memory site—rich in its materiality, functional and freighted with symbolism.

Initial visions of American Jews as immigrants produced another important visual heritage, one grounded in portraiture and an understanding of photography as a form of social work. The pathbreaking documentary photographer Lewis Wickes Hine initiated the process with his influential studies of immigrants arriving at Ellis Island. Born in Oshkosh, Wisconsin, Hine traveled to New York City to teach the children of middle-class German-Jewish immigrants at the Ethical Culture School started by the religious reformer Felix Adler. Hine visited Ellis Island in 1905, a peak year when 129,000 Jews arrived in the United States.[25] He sought to capture the experience of immigrants entering the promised land (the title given one of his photographs). "There are two things I wanted to do," he later explained. "I wanted to show the things that had to be corrected. I wanted to show the things that had to be appreciated."[26] The trips to Ellis Island were among his first efforts to use a camera to tell a story. "Whether it be a painting or a photograph, the picture is the symbol that brings one into close touch with reality," Hine told a social work conference in 1909. "In fact," he admitted, "it is often more effective than the reality would have been, because, in the picture, the non-essential and conflicting interests have been eliminated."[27] Hine's photographs do more than capture moments of passage into the New World; they bring to consciousness a mixed sense of elation and anxiety regarding what would be required to pass into that new American world. As a result they also prompt ways of thinking about Jewish immigrants within the narrative framework of such a passage and such a passing.

The individuality and directness of the portrait impress the viewer of *Young Russian Jewess at Ellis Island*, 1905. Although Hine did not record her name (probably because he could not communicate with her through speech), his camera captured her personal identity. In that sense his photograph assimilates her to the classic ideology of American individualism. She participates through Hine in that formative American tale that imagines a young person poised on the threshold, ready to make her way in the world and to reinvent herself.[28] Framed by a half halo of light from the large windows on the second floor of the main building at Ellis Island, the young Jewish immigrant exudes a sense of hope and promise. Her oval face surrounded by a dark kerchief is illuminated as though it echoes the architecture. We notice her dark eyes, long nose, high forehead, full lips,

Lewis W. Hine, *Young Russian Jewess at Ellis Island*, 1905. Courtesy Photography Collection, Miriam and Ira D. Wallach Division of Art, Prints and Photographs, New York Public Library, Astor, Lenox and Tilden Foundations.

firm chin, and serious demeanor. Behind her jut the steel railings that guided thousands of immigrants each day through the maze of tests that led to admission to the United States—or rejection. Her straightforward gaze evokes the Christian journalist Hutchins Hapgood's description of "the modern type" of immigrant Jewish women: "They have in personal character many virtues called masculine, are simple and straightforward and intensely serious, and do not 'bank' in any way on the fact that they are women!" Hapgood had American middle-class women in mind as the norm when he explained how a Jewish immigrant woman behaved: "Such a woman would feel insulted if her escort were to pick up her handkerchief or in any way suggest a politeness growing out of the difference in sex."[29] Hine's young woman in the photograph has yet to make it to the Lower East Side where Hapgood might have encountered her. Yet she seems prepared for the journey before her. She is a gripping image of strength and vulnerability, endurance and determination.

Hine possessed a "liberal progressive outlook," but he saw himself less as an artist than as a "working photographer performing a certain kind of cultural (and political) labor." For Hine words and pictures go together, as they did for Riis. But Hine is interested in a larger reform project than decent housing, though he too required "an activated public opinion." Alan Trachtenberg has written about Hine that he seemed engaged in presenting images "through which social information might become the viewer's own concrete experience—not facts 'out there,' in a distant realm, or facts to excite pity, but visual facts as the occasion for awakening the viewer's awareness of and imaginative empathy with the pictured others, and thus the viewer's own social being."[30] If Trachtenberg is right, Hine was inviting those who saw his photographs to imagine Jewish immigrants as integral to their own social realm. These pictures of Jewish immigrants, personal and immediate, demand an empathetic response to the subject's humanity as a way of acknowledging our own. By affixing descriptive labels on his immigrant subjects through his photographic titles, Hine brings individual Jews into his contemporary American world. His camera provides a kind of intimacy. He tells Jewish immigrant stories through his photographs, making them American stories.

Forty years later Henri Cartier-Bresson, a French Catholic photographer visiting New York City, where he had previously studied with the modernist Jewish photographer Paul Strand (a student of Hine), went to the docks to observe immigrants entering the United States. World War II had just ended. The losses of the Holocaust were fresh and raw.

Born in 1908 in Chanteloup, Seine-en-Marne, the eldest son of a prosperous textile manufacturer, Cartier-Bresson refused to enter his father's business and set off to become a photojournalist. After studying with Strand and visiting Mexico, he returned to France to work for the communist newspaper *Ce Soir*. In 1940 he joined the French army to fight the Nazis but was captured. He spent three years as a prisoner of war in Germany before escaping in 1943. Then he joined the Resistance and used his camera to document conditions of soldiers and sailors as well as to capture emotions of rage and exhilaration after the liberation of Paris.[31]

Cartier-Bresson emphasized the importance of the living moment. Photography, "an instantaneous expression, both sensory and intellectual," he wrote, not only is "an expression of the world in visual terms" but also is "a perpetual quest and interrogation." The photographer "cannot be a passive spectator; he can be really lucid only if he is caught up in the event."[32]

On that day in 1946 Cartier-Bresson was caught up in the event of homecoming. Homecoming, as the critic Max Kozloff points out, "is a composite of delayed union and remembered absence, precipitated in the rustle of bodies."[33] But this photograph is more than that, for American Jews bring to the image specific associations of a war waged against European Jews and the knowledge of how few mothers and sons survived to embrace again. As Claude Cookman writes persuasively, "While Cartier-Bresson shows a preference for decontextualizing his photographs, the historical contexts behind his work enrich personal interpretation and formal appreciation."[34] Certainly historical consciousness enhances the power of this photograph. Yet of course it is impossible to know whether Jews are pictured or even if the photo portrays a mother and son embracing. Indeed Jewish mothers and fathers were more likely to have sent their sons and daughters away from a Europe embroiled in war than to have fled leaving their children behind. Nevertheless it remains extraordinarily difficult not to read a redemptive possibility into this embrace.

Cartier-Bresson was not particularly interested in Jews, rather in the

Henri Cartier-Bresson, *New York*, 1946. © Magnum Photos.

human story at "the decisive moment."[35] His photograph of refugees entering the port of New York taken in 1946 presents an image of displacement and people in transit. Perhaps because American Jews have yet to integrate survivors' stories into American Jewish history, focusing instead on their lives in Europe and on the failure of American Jews to rescue more of them, we have not seen in such a photograph a liminal passage from an old life to a new one.[36] The image is arresting in its ability to remind us of the religious dimensions of this transition: pain, fear, hope, relief, and love. Most of the figures are blurred; only the woman and crying man are crisp. We notice her black-gloved hand, emphasizing her gesture of affection. We see his grief, his hand holding a white handkerchief to his eyes to staunch his tears. Between the two runs a railing, barely visible. Behind them are the blurred faces of men, women, and children, most wearing hats and warm coats. Above the pair floats a man's outstretched arm, waving to a familiar face in the crowd we cannot see. And one man in glasses on the right watches the scene of homecoming as we do, reminding us of how we peer into this terribly private reunion held in public. Cartier-Bresson brings us close to the couple. We do not look down, nor do we stand apart. We feel almost as though we could touch them. The intimacy, the press of the crowd, and the sense of anticipation convey a powerful story of longing and desire.

We interpret these two photographs in light of the history of American Jews as immigrants. The American Jewish story is one of transitions, of ruptures and reconstructions, of escapes and arrivals. Immigrant and Jew go hand in hand, a familiar narrative of displacement and struggle. We count the generations removed from immigration: children of immigrants are the second generation, while their children, native-born of native-born parents, the ones privileged to know their immigrant grandparents, are the third generation. (Often neither immigrants nor their children ever knew grandparents who remained behind in Europe.) We divide the history of American Jews into periods based on immigration, with German Jews located midway between Sephardic Jews and the more numerous Eastern European Jews. Thus it makes sense that those photos of migrants, whether refugees or immigrants, set some of the critical dimensions for Jewish self-perceptions.

Although a still photograph can show only a slice of space and a sliver of time, nevertheless it can catalyze our imaginations. How can this be? First, each photo calls out to us: "Look at this!" And as if to make up for everything that it cannot show us, a photo grants us permission to stare—closely and at length.[37] Second, no photograph is an island. Many photos—both amateur snapshots and professional pictures—exist in explicit or implied dialogue with other photographs. That conversation among photos allows us to view versions of Jewish study—for example, Riis's *Talmud School in Hester Street Tenement*, Eagle's *Yeshiva*, and Capa's *Hebrew Lesson*—as engaged in related efforts to portray a core Jewish practice in American cities.

Photography's power to preserve images of the past allows us also to see the Lower East Side. The neighborhood's absorbing legacy lives in Jewish collective memory, and Jews conjure its history through tastes, smells, and sounds, but especially sights. It is nearly impossible to think about the Lower East Side without seeing its streets filled with people. The neighborhood often pulses with rich and vibrant associations. Because the experience of the Lower East Side is as much created as it is lived, we cannot imagine the streets of the Lower East Side apart from a century of photography that has frozen them in our minds. Jews summoned up images of the Lower East Side that recounted their past.[38]

The historian Beth Wenger argues that in the 1920s the Lower East Side ceased to be a center of Jewish population and activity and became instead "a primary site of Jewish memory and a physical space for the invention of Jewish identity in America." American Jews came to forge a collective consciousness for themselves through the Lower East Side, developing a narrative of arrival, suffering, adaptation, and eventual triumph. As Wenger writes, the neighborhood became "a living reminder of an idealized immigrant world as well as a mirror of the past that reflected the extent of Jewish progress." Nostalgia served to shape American Judaism in the making and allowed Jews to articulate a common account of their urban origins. The "neighborhood represented poverty but also the possibility for upward mobility; it testified to the existence of a vibrant, ethnic culture but also to the ability of Jews to adapt to American society; it enshrined the flavor of the Old World but also housed stores and businesses serving the new American consumer; it celebrated the rapid acculturation of American Jews but also expressed the doubts and frustrations that accompanied the drive for Americanization."[39]

One way to understand the iconic power of immigrant Jewish neighborhoods as well as their impact on American understandings of urban life is to contrast two American versions of the "ghetto." One by Hapgood dates from the turn of the twentieth century and derives from visits he made to New York's Lower East Side guided by Abraham Cahan, a Jewish journalist who would subsequently make his career as editor of the *Forverts*, the extraordinarily popular Yiddish daily with a circulation reaching a quarter of a million at its peak.[40] The other, by the Jewish sociologist Louis Wirth, dates from the 1920s, after immigration had been restricted, and derives from his observations of Chicago's Maxwell Street neighborhood.[41] In both cases Jewish streets stimulate reflections on urbanism and prompt considerations on how Jews imbue city neighborhoods with distinctive meanings. Wirth's view of the ghetto portrays the immigrant area as pathological, in contrast to Hapgood's modern cosmopolitanism and creative ferment. Wirth's sociological concept with its psychological dimensions entered linguistic usage as descriptive of oppressive urban society and the dangers of segregation. Hapgood's more romantic version of the ghetto that depicted its cultural energies eventually produced nostalgic evocations of the Lower East Side as a heritage site, an authentic Jewish place in America, the "most popular locus of American Jewish memory."[42]

Not until a new generation of photographers born and raised on the Lower East Side picked up cameras during the Depression and the 1940s did the area's image become more richly variegated. These Jewish photographers, including Rebecca Lepkoff and Walter Rosenblum, pictured their own neighborhood. They saw its space as intimates not visitors. "I didn't even have to think," Lepkoff later claimed. "I just went outside, and there were the streets of my mother, of me."[43] Lepkoff's recollection makes a gendered claim to the streets and the neighborhood. Recognition of her achievement in part reflected a new awareness about the "world of our mothers" that emerged in response to the 1976 publication of Irving Howe's monumental *World of Our Fathers: The Journey of the East European Jews to America and the Life They Found and Made* and the rise of a Jewish feminist movement. That same year saw the publication of

The Jewish Woman in America, a book that helped to initiate historical explorations of the roles and responsibilities of Jewish women.[44]

Both Lepkoff and Rosenblum were taking pictures of home, not some foreign place. Beginning in the 1930s young Jewish men and women with cameras began documenting the world of their youth. Examining the eye-level humanism of their street photography shows how their images rejected the popular architectural bias and romantic style that had dominated urban photographic representations. Instead their photographs demand a particular type of "participatory viewing" and invite narrative improvisation.

Young Jewish photographers associated with the New York Photo League, like Lepkoff and Rosenblum, found themselves tuning in to the way street life organized itself in a shifting matrix of sight lines and body language. They walked the streets like flaneurs on a mission. The enlightenment they pursued was distantly indebted to Kant but also to Hillel the Elder. They were out for themselves, but not only for themselves; they would *not* wait; and they *would* explore the larger text of the city before them. Sometimes, like acolytes of Diogenes, Photo League photographers aimed their cameras as if they were flashlights. They went for the trifecta: the true, the good, and the beautiful. At the Photo League, "artwork," in philosopher John Dewey's terms, amounted to *tikkun olam* by bricoleurs, on a quest to gather, per Jewish mystical tradition, the scattered sparks of light from a broken universe to repair the world.[45]

Walter Rosenblum grew up on the streets of the Lower East Side. He lived its poverty in a three-room cold-water flat in an environment of "religious orthodoxy, economic instability and familial love."[46] Rosenblum nonetheless managed to attend City College for a couple of years. He joined the New York Photo League in 1938, when he was still a teenager, and discovered his voice through a camera. The Photo League, established in 1936, brought Rosenblum into a setting both Jewish and American, deeply engaged with left-wing politics and profoundly committed to photography as a progressive practice. Rosenblum became actively involved, editing the newsletter *PhotoNotes* until he entered military service during World War II. His Photo League was dedicated to education and socially engaged photography. Along with other league members he rejected "bourgeois" practices: nude, landscape, and still-life photography. Photographers at the league organized themselves thematically into feature groups to represent the everyday life of poor and unemployed people, both mirroring them back to themselves and revealing their lives outward to the larger world. Rosenblum joined one of the feature groups, teaming up with others to document the neighborhood around Pitt Street, Lower East Side blocks he knew very well.

Rosenblum started taking pictures eager to change the world by documenting the lives of ordinary working people and making their experiences accessible to all Americans. "If you are photographing someone, you owe them a print," he explained in an interview in 1992. "[S]omeone would say to me, why are you taking my picture? . . . I would say 'I think you look terrific, that's why I'm taking your picture,' . . . So I always gave out pictures to the people I photographed on Pitt Street."[47] As he said defensively about his fellow photographers at the Photo League who were also taking pictures of the Lower East Side and other gritty urban neighborhoods, "We're not tourists spying on the quaint mannerisms of the people."[48] Commerce didn't interest them as it had attracted outsiders fascinated with pushcart markets. In any case the city had built indoor markets in the mid-1930s, forcing many of the pushcart vendors off the streets.[49] But Lepkoff and Rosenblum also chose to photograph different blocks than had previous photographers. They chose some of the poorest ones, including Pitt and Cherry, rather than bustling commercial streets like Hester, Orchard, Delancey, and Grand.

Like Lepkoff, Rosenblum documented his own world. "I realized," he later said, "that I worked best when I was photographing something or someone I loved and that through my photographs I could pay them homage."[50] His photograph *Gypsy and Vegetable Dealer, Pitt Street, Lower East Side, New York City, 1938*, part of the Pitt Street Project, reveals the interactions of neighbors, the mix of commerce and housing, the conversations that occurred from the stoop to the street and through the open windows. This diversity represents clearly a poor urban milieu where distinctions between public and private space blur. A woman sits with her sewing by the window where the light is good and converses with a bareheaded man standing at the entry to the fruit and vegetable store, located several steps below street level. The conversation has caught the attention of another man, dressed in suit and hat despite the heat, and he

Walter Rosenblum, *Gypsy and Vegetable Dealer, Pitt Street, Lower East Side, New York City*, 1938. © Walter Rosenblum. Courtesy Naomi Rosenblum.

leans forward to listen. A mother and child slowly make their way down the stoop's steps. Watching it all is a man, likely the owner of the shop, sitting on a chair in the gutter. He has removed his worn sweater and appears relaxed and poised, waiting for customers. Above a metal gate leading to a passageway between the two tenements a barely legible sign advertises in Yiddish and English. The scene is ordinary yet intimate. A snapshot of everyday close encounters, it captures a vision of a neighborhood sustained by quotidian exchanges.

The view from the rooftop looks completely different. It is summertime in the city. The two young men have taken off their shirts; one has rolled up his pants, and the other wears shorts. The four women are more modestly dressed, having removed only their shoes. Nonetheless, one woman, with her back to us, has exposed her legs, standing on tiptoe to lean on the building's ledge. The photographer has interrupted this group on *Tar Beach*, the moniker applied to sunbathing possibilities

Walter Rosenblum, *Tar Beach, Pitt Street, Lower East Side, New York City*, 1938. © Walter Rosenblum. Courtesy Naomi Rosenblum.

on New York City rooftops. The couple lying down ignores his presence, but the other young man turns toward him. Despite the intrusion Rosenblum's photo invites us to taste the freedom of the roof. Lying on a blanket placed over newspapers to protect it from the tarpaper, young men and women enjoy the pleasure of their own company and avoid the watchful presence of adults on the streets below. The city, laid out before them and especially the bridge, appears beautiful from such a perspective.

Down on the street is an intergenerational world of mothers and fathers, daughters and sons. Lepkoff's photograph of Cherry Street pictures a scene of familiarly coordinate gestures. A child of immigrant Jews, Lepkoff also grew up on the Lower East Side. Studying to be a dancer, she learned about photography through the New York Photo League. Her photographs often capture movement or, as in this case, the pause for conversation that knits the fabric of a poor neighborhood. Lepkoff

Rebecca Lepkoff, *Cherry Street*, ca. 1940s. © Rebecca Lepkoff.
Courtesy Howard Greenberg Gallery, New York.

snapped this picture of her neighbors standing in front of her own tenement building. These are photographs of Jews, but the observer must bring that knowledge to the images. Rosenblum and Lepkoff allow us to see these residents of the Lower East Side as human beings without any other identities.

This is a poor neighborhood as witnessed by the building's worn façade and blank windows and the laundry flapping in the cool air, but dismal living conditions do not intrigue Lepkoff. Pay attention, she suggests, to the people, to the human interactions of the street. Her photograph invites us to look at gestures, what she called "the choreography of the movement of the streets,"[51] things she might observe as a dancer: the crossed legs and relaxed posture of the man lounging against the tenement door frame, the clasped hands and slightly bent heads of the two older women talking, the sprawl of children playing unconcerned that they are blocking the stairs, and of course the ubiquitous American practice of standing with hands in pockets. Lepkoff's photo also comments implicitly on urban relationships between public and private spaces. All that laundry hanging between the tenement windows across a vacant lot that everyone on the street can see reminds us of a type of familiarity that exists on city streets, especially in poor neighborhoods. Similarly the conversations we cannot hear—between a woman pushing a baby carriage and a man, between two older women, and even among the three young children playing—suggest a kind of urban sound track. Younger American-born women and men freely socialize on these streets, as do boys and girls, counter to social practices prevalent in the early part of the twentieth century.[52]

Lepkoff's picture highlights a range of particular yet common interactions. Her photos work in implicit contrast to omissions or exclusions: out-of-date stereotypes of the Lower East Side as an immigrant neighborhood associated with Yiddish culture and ragtag small-scale commerce. As the historian Suzanne Wasserman emphasizes, "the street and the neighborhood were very much about family."[53] There is no explicit political agenda here, no reformer's call to eradicate the slums. Rather Lepkoff asks us to look at the streets of the Lower East Side as common ground, a place of city life, of poverty but also dignity. Her photograph represents in visual terms Wenger's articulation of American Jews' nostalgic narrative, possessing all of the coordinates of urban community.

Like Lepkoff, Bella Spewack, a twenty-three-year-old reporter for the socialist *New York Call*, took snapshots of the streets of her childhood. Only she wielded a pen, not a camera, when in 1922 she wrote a powerful memoir of her years growing up on the Lower East Side. The memoir, not published until after her death, describes a world far removed from the successful career and marriage Bella enjoyed with her husband and coauthor of plays, Sam Spewack. But Florence Howe's decision to publish the memoir in 1995 under the Feminist Press imprint attests to the meaning she saw in Spewack's unpublished account for another generation. Spewack's snapshots of a past urban childhood enticed contemporary American Jews, especially women, to revisit the world of their grandmothers and to integrate that distant time with its urban Judaism into their own self-understanding as American Jews. Through such pictures of the past and their imaginative potential, American Jews reclaimed a version of urban Judaism for themselves.

Spewack had arrived in the United States as Bella Cohen, a three-year-old from Transylvania, traveling with her mother, a divorced woman. Aptly titled *Streets*, the memoir chronicled her many moves from one block to another, each move measuring her mother's fortunes: Cannon Street, where they first lived after entering the United States; Stanton Street, where they made their initial move to better their lives; Lewis Street, where her half-brothers were born and her mother's disastrous second marriage played itself out; Goersk Street, where they retreated even further in poverty; and finally First Avenue, where they first lived outside the Jewish Lower East Side. Each address encapsulated a snapshot of her life. Moving from one block to another charted her path into American Jewish womanhood. Her account of growing up vividly describes the poverty she endured as well as her desire for beauty, cleanliness, and fun. Her mother's aspirations for her kept her from teenage employment and permitted her to attend high school, highly unusual for a young woman from such a poverty-stricken background.[54]

Bella Spewack recounted few elements of religious life as a young girl. Her Lower East Side bore few external marks of Jewish religious practice, but its milieu entered the American Jewish religious imagination as a formative site *and* a place to flee. In Bella's case she escaped through public education. Other Jews would find different means to climb out of poverty. They would tell different stories, but the arc of self-invention would endure. In this American Jews borrowed from European modernity, selecting themes of self-making and situating them in the city.

The Jewish photographers gathered around the Photo League extended the urban documentary tradition and identified Jews with city life. These Jewish photographers no longer portrayed American Jews as immigrants; now they were New Yorkers, with all of the toughness and resilience the city was famous for. The postures, dress, movement, and drama of their lives played out against a rough backdrop of brownstone and steel, iron railings and paved streets.

Rosenblum's photograph *Girl on a Swing* conveys her pleasure at surmounting the strictures of her world. She imagines herself soaring high on a swing, not in the shadow of the bridge but up in the air reaching its heights. Taken as part of the Pitt Street Project, *Girl on a Swing* captures the pleasure of motion. Its point of view reflects an understanding of urban life as filled with potential. The girl on the swing does indeed transform the space of steel and concrete looming above her. Although we can't hear it, cars, trucks, and trains on the Manhattan Bridge are roaring overhead. American Jews recognized this world unfolding and saw themselves and judged their progress toward a better life through these photographs.

That better life arrived in subsequent decades when Jews moved out of iconic immigrant neighborhoods and even out of the industrial cities of the Northeast and Midwest for new metropolises in the booming Sunbelt. Perhaps no place vied more aggressively for recognition than Los Angeles, the second city after World War II for both the United States and American Jews. Like New York, Los Angeles possessed a booming entertainment industry that broadcast images throughout the country. Jews worked in this industry—both the movies and television—and discovered a prosperity and well-being that they had scarcely imagined possible back east. But adjusting to life lived out of doors in a beachfront

Walter Rosenblum, *Girl on a Swing, Pitt Street, Lower East Side, New York City*, 1938. © Walter Rosenblum. Courtesy Naomi Rosenblum.

city with palm trees and abundant sunshine required learning to see a different culture.

Max Yavno made the move to Los Angeles from New York after the war. He had grown up in the Bronx, attended City College, and even completed a year of graduate study at Columbia University Business School. But he taught himself photography. Persuaded to return to the New York Photo League as president, he studied with Aaron Siskind, his "spiritual mentor," working with him on two documentary projects, *Harlem Document* and *The Most Crowded Street in the World*. At the Photo League Yavno mastered the art of printing by sharing the darkroom with Conseulo Kanaga. He was fortunate to work with Hallie Flanagan, the director of the WPA Theater Project. She sent Yavno to photograph real streets to serve as "first sketches for sets and backdrops." This connection introduced Yavno to ways of seeing the city as a potential stage set for performances. Married at nineteen and divorced four years later, Yavno served in the military and thought of himself as a photographer. When he arrived in Los Angeles he began taking pictures of people as he had in New York. But the photographs portrayed a different world.[55]

Yavno's photo *Muscle Beach*, depicting a section of Venice, California, presents a radically different vision from that of Rosenblum's *Girl on a Swing* with its singular sense of urban freedom. Here instead are masses of youth eager to perform and compete for attention. We stand behind a couple wearing bathing suits, watching in amazement as muscular young men and women throw themselves around chinning bars. The man has his arm around the woman, as if to ensure everyone recognizes that they are a pair. A crowd of eager observers stands and sits, enjoying the display of athletic ability. Men toss women high into the air and balance them stretched out on a single upraised hand. Others scramble to get into the action. Yavno's vision of the exuberance also captures a sign advertising "PHYSICAL SERVICES" in large print, and then "tumbling, balancing, gymnastics, adagio," promising a "modern clean safe" gym at "reasonable rates" for "all ages." This is a very different urban world, where physical culture explodes on the beach in front of stores selling snow cones and colas. In the background are taller multifamily houses. It would take Jewish newcomers a while to assimilate into such a different urban society and to make a home for themselves before they

Max Yavno, *Muscle Beach*, 1949. Collection Center for Creative Photography. © 1998 Center for Creative Photography, The University of Arizona Foundation.

would be able to produce those powerful snapshots that narrate an account of American Jewish space.

In the 1990s Lauren Greenfield, who grew up in Los Angeles and went east to attend college at Harvard University, returned to the city with her camera and a desire to understand her childhood world of privilege. "Los Angeles is where I grew up and formed many of my ideas about myself and the world," she explains. It was a world of privilege and affluence. Although as a "documentarian" she had photographed other cultures, now she sought to comprehend her own wealthy Jewish milieu. "By exploring my own culture, I could begin with a level of access and understanding impossible elsewhere after the most extensive research and fieldwork." Greenfield echoes both Lepkoff and Rosenblum in her rationale for picturing her own environment. But since Greenfield left Los Angeles to attend college, her most vivid memories of the city revolved around high school. The four-year photography project that became *Fast Forward* started at her own private high school but then took her to public schools and sections of the city she did not know: South Central and East Los Angeles. Like any big city Los Angeles promoted homogeneity in its neighborhoods, divided by race and class.[56]

In her book Greenfield focuses on a loss of innocence and a kind of reciprocity that exists between Hollywood and teenagers. On the one hand Hollywood exerts enormous influence on youth coming of age in the city; on the other hand local teenagers occasionally inspire producers of popular culture to try something new. She also pays attention to how religion continues to shape American Jewish identity in the city, focusing on the rising importance of extravagant rites of passage for both girls and boys. If bar mitzvah parties emerged in the mid-twentieth century as sites of urban improvisation and Jewish exuberance (and occasional excess), after the rise of second-wave feminism in the 1960s Jewish girls increasingly celebrated a bat mitzvah just like their brothers' bar mitzvahs.[57]

Greenfield's photograph *Young Girls in Party Dresses with Professionally Done Hair at a Bat Mitzvah Party at the 20th Century Fox Movie Studio Commissary in West Los Angeles, California, 1992* depicts preadolescent youngsters unsure of themselves. All dressed up in sophisticated bare-shouldered dresses and wearing pearl or gold necklaces, they talk, we imagine, about what to do and what will be. One chews on her golden heart necklace, her chubby hand with its red nail polish pressed against her chest. Another one, shorter than the other two girls, listens with a worried look on her face. We can't see the third girl, only her beautiful multicolored bow in her hair, but we assume she is talking since the other two appear to be listening. Behind them cars are parked, while the white line demarcating one side of the road from another runs between the girls. The party is going on elsewhere. Having no sidewalk where they might gather to discuss matters, they stand in the street, albeit a private one in the public city. Growing up in the shadow of Hollywood, Greenfield sees a "quest for notoriety" as a rite of passage.[58] This is hardly the transmission of Jewish culture pictured so optimistically by Eagle, though there is no doubt that Judaism is being passed on here to another generation. But Greenfield's photo makes us ponder what is being shared, what is conveyed in this late twentieth-century version of urban Judaism.

Reflecting on the rounds of bar mitzvahs he attended the year he turned thirteen, the poet Milton Klonsky (1921–81), who grew up in Brighton Beach, next door to Coney Island in Brooklyn, recalls, "I remember the whole time as a continual bazaar of parties and celebrations. Every other week, one after the other, I saw my friends rise up and declare their manhood while the rest of us sat in the back rows, apart

Lauren Greenfield, *Young Girls in Party Dresses with Professionally Done Hair at a Bat Mitzvah Party at the 20th Century Fox Movie Studio Commissary in West Los Angeles, California*, 1992. © Lauren Greenfield. Courtesy Lauren Greenfield / INSTITUTE.

from the relatives, giggling and throwing spitballs, with our *yamelkas* slanted on the side of our heads at a sharp angle." Klonsky's was an urban working-class version of coming of age as a Jewish boy in the 1930s. With the religious ritual of a bar mitzvah a Jewish boy ascended into adulthood, theoretically accepted as a morally responsible member of the Jewish community. "[W]e were admitted," Klonsky observed. "But where?" he queried. "For what had we been prepared?" "Certainly not for the ritual despair of our forefathers," he answered, ". . . although we knew we could never resign from the old contract with the past, our long history bonded by memory and always annealed in the present."[59]

In short, there was no escape from the claims of American Judaism. But Klonsky's was a new generation. What, he wondered, "was our point of view"? What, we might paraphrase, was the point of view of an American Jew, born and bred in New York City? "What, in short," Klonsky wrote, "was the angle?" And he replied, "A New York question, rhetorical, rebounding from its own answer! It was New York we were prepared for, and New York, half-Jewish, which took us in. New York!

Ghetto of Eden! We go back always where we came from, in memory, to and from ourselves. The things that made us what we are made you."[60]

American Judaism acquired its shape in this older Jewish urban milieu, those "ghettos of Eden" in Klonsky's evocative phrase. Jews lived it on the streets as well as in their homes. The naturalness and apparent authenticity of urban Judaism, which blurred boundaries between public and private space, particularly provoked nostalgia among those Jews who chose to be Jewish in the suburbs largely in private. The density of neighborhood life, the evocative qualities of streets, their sights and their smells, the presence of Jewish stores and shops, the need to negotiate hostile neighbors, and the diversity of Jews situate Judaism within a strikingly different milieu than the one familiar to suburban Jews. In the suburbs, as Riv-Ellen Prell has argued, affiliation, usually with a synagogue, replaced a spatialized identity typical of city living.[61] In the 1980s and 1990s as the streets of many American cities no longer boasted signs of a Jewish presence, snapshots occupied their place in the imagination of American Jews. Through images American Jews consumed versions of their history, creating memory sites that added depth, details, and difference to a Jewish environment increasingly seen as bland, formal, institutionalized, and homogeneous.

Yet of all the photographs that American Jews came to adopt as central to their narrative self-understanding, none can compete with one by Alfred Stieglitz (1864–1946), an American Jew who never confronted poverty. Ironically the most powerful, certainly the most iconic of American Jewish images comes from a creative misreading of a famous Stieglitz photograph that pictures a liminal moment aboard a ship.

In 1907 Stieglitz, photographer, American-born son of prosperous German Jewish immigrants, married gentleman of leisure, took a trip to Europe aboard the *Kaiser Wilhelm II*. Although born in Hoboken in 1864 and educated as a child in New York City, Stieglitz was no stranger to Europe. He traveled there frequently and had studied photochemistry in Germany in the 1880s when his family moved there. Of his first camera, which he bought in Berlin in 1883, he wrote, "It fascinated me, first as a passion, then as an obsession." Having grown up in a secularizing household that had jettisoned Judaism, Stieglitz found religion in photography. "The camera was waiting for me by predestination," he wrote, "and I took to it as a musician takes to a piano or a painter to canvas. I found I was master of the elements, that I could work miracles; that I could do things which had never before been done."[62] Such religious language reflected his profound commitment to the power of photography. When Stieglitz returned in 1890 to New York City from his years in Europe, he came as a man with a mission. Shocked at the low regard of photography as a popular hobby akin to bicycling, he determined to change Americans' attitudes.

Over the course of several decades Stieglitz would set up a "photographic scene" in New York City to promote photography as an art, but one endowed with spiritual dimensions. Both his gallery and journal, though relatively short-lived, exerted exceptional influence in establishing parameters for seeing photographs, which would come to include small gallery exhibition, fine-art publication, and eventually museum acquisition. This was a far cry from Eastman Kodak's slogan "You press the button, we do the rest" that accompanied its introduction of the box camera in 1888.[63] Stieglitz developed a credo: "I was born in Hoboken," he declared. "I am an American. Photography is my passion. The search for Truth my obsession."[64] He "stood at the center of a movement which sought to produce a new American art and culture, a movement openly critical of the aggressive commercialism, hypocritical moralism and empty conventionality of the reigning culture," writes Trachtenberg.[65] Stieglitz considered immigration of masses of impoverished men and women, including two million Jews, from Southern and Eastern Europe to work in factories as part of this crass commercial America. The plight of hundreds of thousands of Jewish immigrants fleeing persecution and poverty in Russia did not particularly move him, an attitude common among other American-born and well-established children of a prior wave of Jewish immigration.

But on this 1907 trip across the Atlantic Stieglitz found the nouveau-riche company in the first-class cabins boring. So he wandered "off alone to look over a railing at the steerage-class passengers. There he experienced a new kind of epiphany, seeing in the scene a 'picture of shapes, and underlying it, a new vision that held me,'" writes the photo historian Joel Smith. Stieglitz needed "to rush back to the stateroom for his camera, which had only one plate left; he knew that if anyone moved, 'the picture I saw would no longer exist.'" As Smith points out, "Stieglitz used these literally fabulous features in his narrative—a hero's lone quest, the retrieval of his charmed implement, the exhaustion of all resources—in order to compress all the story's drama into the single act of exposing his negative."[66] Smith suggests that after that photograph, which Stieglitz subsequently named *The Steerage*, the photographer's "real subject would be what he called 'the living moment.'"[67]

The Steerage would subsequently acquire iconic status for American Jews not as an image of migrants returning to their homes in Europe but of immigrants en route to enter the United States.[68] Despite his evident distance from his foreign subjects and his perspective looking down on them, Stieglitz's photograph captivates viewers. "The social extremes evident in the picture," writes Hans-Michael Koetzle, ". . . were the trigger, not the goal of his pictorial exploration. Stieglitz sought not to penetrate, but to aestheticize, the world by means of photography." The complex play of shapes, of hats and laundry, of angled stairs and smokestack "boldly anticipated what came to be called the New Objectivity in photography."[69] *The Steerage* was a "straight" photograph by a master of dreamy pictorialism. In fact, Stieglitz used this photograph to foreshadow his own "eventual escape from his family, and from his leisure-class identity."[70] He embedded a personal story in the image of men and women in transit from one world to another. This metaphoric interpretation may in part be what subsequently drew American Jews to the photo.

The photograph captures a crowded upper deck of a ship filled with men and women traveling second class and a slightly less crowded lower deck where women predominate. In the middle a chain-link gangplank forms a kind of bridge. On the right steps heading down from one deck to the other can be seen, while on the left a smokestack slants upward in a reverse angle from the steps. Our glance gravitates to one man's round white straw hat with black band and then follows his gaze down to the deck below, where a white shawl, with two black stripes, similarly holds us. Women, their heads covered with scarves, cradle babies in their arms as children loll around. The picture invites us to imagine an epic unfolding before our eyes. Despite its straight style and geometry of shapes, it appears to tell a classic tale, capturing a liminal time in transit from

Alfred Stieglitz, *The Steerage*, 1907. © 2013 Georgia O'Keefe Museum / Artist Rights Society (ARS), New York.

New World to Old or Old World to New, the passengers unaware of what awaits them on arrival.

When *The Steerage*, 1907 is reproduced, as it often is, it invites identification by American Jews of the third-class passengers as Jews.[71] The year marked one of the high points of Jewish immigration to the United States when over 148,000 entered, most of them at Ellis Island.[72] Relatively few Jews ever returned to Europe. Their rate of return, estimated between 7 and 15 percent, was among the lowest of all immigrant groups arriving in the United States, reducing the likelihood that Stieglitz photographed Jews.[73] Yet although Stieglitz's photograph actually portrays the failure of immigration since these men, women, and children are returning to Europe, his skilled pictorial narrative allows us to perceive Jewish immigrants, even to identify the passengers as Jews by misreading the shawl with its two black stripes as a tallit, a prayer shawl. We imagine that the men and women on the deck below are about to enter America, rather than leaving it, either denied admission or part of a regular pattern of return migration.[74] Stieglitz's renown as a photographer, his importance in shaping American photography in the early decades of the twentieth century, his acknowledged Jewish identity, and the photograph's title as well as its evident power and popularity conspire to make this image an iconic one of Jewish immigration. It is one of the first portrayals of "Jews as immigrants" and one of the earliest ways American Jews came to see themselves: they were participating in an epic exodus from Europe to a new promised land.

These images of American Jews trace a curious arc. From poor immigrant outsiders, crowded together in urban slums, a people in transit whose stories can be understood as American stories, Jews are portrayed as quintessential New Yorkers, poor but savvy, drawing strength from their public presence on the city's streets. Then in the postwar period Jewish photographers transformed the heritage of street photography and social documentary, of slum spectacle and exotic otherness. Living in very different cities they sought to explain their own prosperous milieu and to figure out what story they wished to tell through their snapshots. Viewing these photographs allows us to glimpse in tangible detail the urban origins of American Judaism, its heterogeneity, multiplicity, and complexity.

CONCLUSION

The departure of Jews for the suburbs in the 1950s and 1960s coincided with a burst of historical writing on Jews and American cities. These histories of the Jews of Baltimore, Cleveland, Rochester, Atlanta, Portland, Chicago, Buffalo, Columbus, and Los Angeles all shared common features. They usually began with the pioneers, the founding fathers as it were, of the Jewish community. But they quickly shifted focus from these figures to the first institutions, almost inevitably a cemetery. After all Jews did not need any special place to pray, but when Jews died they needed to be buried in sanctified land. From these initial efforts at organizing a community, the histories describe growth and conflict. Newcomers brought both, expanding the community and introducing strife. Synagogues and community centers, old-age homes and orphan asylums, charitable organizations and efforts to defend Jews from discrimination appear as the lineaments of urban community. Progress too is charted as Jews move from older and poorer sections of town to more prosperous areas. Each history describes a kind of arc from simplicity to complexity, from poverty to prosperity, from religious devotion to religious multiplicity, from Yiddish and German culture to English and American culture. And then they stop because the story has been told and because the mobility that enlivens each one eventually leads Jews out of each city.

However, these historical narratives all position American Jews and Judaism as urban stories. They identify Jews through their particular cities—much as synagogues often informally took the name of the streets on which they were located—and argue implicitly that the history of American Jews derives from the urban experience. Yet despite picturing Jews as integral to the history of each city, these accounts emphasize a communal and often insular understanding of American Judaism. This is in some ways ironic since urban experience most often is understood as interethnic, multicultural, and cosmopolitan rather than parochial. Cities as modernizing environments also rarely figure in the depictions of Jews' progression to middle-class respectability. Still these histories remain the repositories of much of the formal memories of American Jews. Even when Jews abandon their hometowns either for suburbs or for other cities like Los Angeles and Miami, they tend to identify themselves with cities as places of origin. The small town or shtetl of Eastern Europe may be the old-country point of reference for American Jews when they think of immigration, but the big city endures as their American starting place, their version of Plymouth Rock.

These chapters have suggested the importance of returning to the urban origins of American Judaism. We need to recognize the significance of cities in forming Jewish religious practices in the United States. Cities have provided more than the locale for American Judaism. Rather Jews have built Judaism into flourishing and ever-changing cityscapes. They have adapted their religious behaviors to the rhythms of urban daily life and forged bonds of belonging through urban patterns of work and residence. In cities the "presence of kin and the overlapping relationship of work, family and a variety of communal organizations" forged a Jewish religious culture that "was diverse, polyvalent, and bounded primarily by space."[1] Jews of all religious stripes and of no particular religious identity mixed together on city streets, and their encounters strengthened new forms o&f Jdaism. This spatial dimension of urban Judaism shaped a lived religion that accommodated pluralism, integrated consumption, and celebrated a democratic ethos that empowered ordinary men and women. It also provided for moments of mobilization and rites of community that often transcended local divisions among Jews and built a collective consciousness of their common commitments.

The density and heterogeneity of city living, its stratification along lines of class, ethnicity, and race and its cosmopolitan concentration of cultural production—especially in the large metropolises—have shaped American Judaism across its diverse movements. From funeral practices to bar and bat mitzvah celebrations, demands of urban living required Jews to innovate. Competition with the lures of the city stimulated Jewish creativity and at times encouraged Jews to bring those performative aspects of the streets and commercial culture into their religious lives. The major movements in American Judaism today—Reform, Conservative, and modern Orthodox Judaism—as well as many of the far smaller movements such as Reconstructionism and even Chabad Lubavitch Hasidism all acquired their distinctive attributes in cities before making the move to the suburbs. While all have flourished in the suburbs by developing substitutions for the simultaneously intimate and anonymous interactions of public urban culture, their historical roots lie in metropolitan life.

NOTES

INTRODUCTION

1. This is not to deny the distinctive experiences of the minority of American Jews who chose to live in small towns. For two excellent histories, see Weissbach, *Jewish Life in Small-Town America*, and Morawska, *Insecure Prosperity*.

2. For a cogent discussion of European urbanization, see Richard I. Cohen, "Urban Visibility and Biblical Visions," 741.

3. There are several excellent general histories of Jews in the United States. Two recent ones are Diner, *The Jews of the United States*, and Sarna, *American Judaism*.

4. See Moore, *City of Promises*.

5. "Jews as a Percentage," n.p.

6. Wald, "Puzzling Politics of American Jews", Goldberg, *Jewish Power*, 30–35.

7. Goren, "Rites of Community."

CHAPTER 1. SYNAGOGUES

1. On the history of synagogues in the United States see Raphael, *Synagogue in America*; Wertheimer, *American Synagogue*.

2. For a good overview of early American Jewish history, see Faber, *Time for Planting*; and Faber, "America's Earliest Jewish Settlers."

3. Ellen Smith, "Strangers and Sojourners."

4. Guttman, "Ezra Stiles."

5. Gruber, *American Synagogues*; Snyder, *Building a Public Judaism*, 1–24; Sarna, *American Judaism*, on synagogue as community.

6. Thanks to Andrew Bush for this observation and comparison with *The Last of the Mohicans*.

7. Emma Lazarus, "In the Jewish Synagogue at Newport," in Schor, *Emma Lazarus*, 265–67.

8. Schor, *Emma Lazarus*, 20.

9. Ibid., 19.

10. I thank Andrew Bush for this insight.

11. See Polland, *Landmark of the Spirit*, for another synagogue that was restored in the twentieth century.

12. The King James Version reads, "But they shall sit every man under his vine and under his fig tree; and none shall make *them* afraid."

13. "From the Newport Congregation to the President of the United States, August 17, 1790," in Schappes, *Documentary History of the Jews*, 79–81.

14. See Naomi W. Cohen, *Jews in Christian America*.

15. Ackermann, "1794 Synagogue," ix.

16. See ibid. Similar trends among Jews can be discerned in other European port cities; see, for example, Dubin, *Port Jews of Habsburg Trieste*.

17. The actual name was Society for the Relief of Orphans and Children of Indigent Parents. Friedman, *These Are Our Children*, 6–7.

18. Moore, "Freedom's Fruits," 11. The following paragraphs are drawn from this article.

19. Quoted in Hagy, *This Happy Land*, 129, emphasis in the original.

20. There is a rich literature on the early Reform movement in Charleston. In addition to specific citations, see Zola, *Isaac Harby of Charleston*; Elzas, *Reformed Society of Israelites*; Liberles, "Conflict over Reforms"; Jick, *Americanization of the Synagogue*; Tarshish, "Charleston Organ Case."

21. Prell, "New Key," 16.

22. Quoted in Hagy, *This Happy Land*, 131, emphasis in the original.

23. Sarna, *American Judaism*, xvii, xviii.

24. Meyer, *Response to Modernity*, 231.

25. Moïse, *Poems of Penina Moïse*.

26. See Ashton, *Rebecca Gratz*. On the Female Hebrew Benevolent Society, see 100–106.

27. Goren, *American Jews*, 43.

28. Rock, *Haven of Liberty*, 113–35.

29. Ibid., 126–30, quote on 129.

30. Ibid., 128–29.

31. See Goldman, "This Is the Gateway to the Lord."

32. Ashton, "Expanding Jewish Life in America."

33. Richard I. Cohen, "Urban Visibility and Biblical Visions," 735.

34. Goren, *American Jews*, 43; Moore, "Social History of American Judaism," 1:295; Richard I. Cohen, "Urban Visibility and Biblical Visions," 735.

35. Moore, "Social History of American Judaism," 1:295; Mendes-Flohr and Reinharz, *Jew in the Modern World*, 532.

36. Bush, "Architecture of Jewish Identity," 192.

37. Quoted in ibid., 195.

38. Braude, *Sisters and Saints.*

39. Goldman, *Beyond the Synagogue Gallery*, 134.

40. Polland and Soyer, *Emerging Metropolis*, 74–79, quotes on 75–76.

41. Lerner, "Narrating the Architecture of Emancipation."

42. Richard I. Cohen, "Urban Visibility and Biblical Visions," 746. He also notes (752) that Jews built these synagogues, such as the one in Pest (later Budapest), even before obtaining equal rights.

43. Polland and Soyer, *Emerging Metropolis*, 73–101, quote on 78.

44. Ibid., 92.

45. Quoted in ibid., 92.

46. Polland, *Landmark of the Spirit*, 100–102.

47. Quoted in Meyer, *Response to Modernity*, 234.

48. Goren, "Public Ceremonies Defining Central Synagogue," 51.

49. Ibid.

50. Ibid., 52–55, quote on 52.

51. Eisenberg, Kahn, and Toll, *Jews of the Pacific Coast*, 52–53.

52. Ibid., 6.

53. Toll, "From Domestic Judaism," 128, 139.

54. Goren, "Jewish New York."

55. Soyer, *Jewish Immigrant Associations*, 60.

56. See Rogow, *Gone to Another Meeting.*

57. Gruber, *American Synagogues*, 27. Gruber also notes the popularity of domes due to the adaptation of Guastavino vaulting, 32, 34.

58. Brinkmann, *Sundays at Sinai*, 2–4, 234–36, quotes on 4.

59. Ibid., 4.

60. Ibid., 123–25, 132, 148–49.

61. Gamm, *Urban Exodus*, 1–2.

62. Mann, *Space and Place*, 131.

63. Hyman, "From City to Suburb," 186–87.

64. Gamm, *Urban Exodus*, 285.

65. Schwartz, *Rabbi's Wife*, 93–101.

66. Quoted in Gamm, *Urban Exodus*, 285.

67. On Detroit, see Rockaway, *Jews of Detroit*; and Bolkosky, *Harmony and Dissonance.*

68. Quoted in Gruber, *American Synagogues*, 62.

69. Quoted in Moore, *To the Golden Cities*, 114, emphasis in the original.

70. Gurock and Schacter, *Modern Heretic and a Traditional Community*, 88–105; Gurock, *Orthodox Jews in America*, 146–47.

71. For a full history of the synagogue center, see Kaufman, *Shul with a Pool.* Kaufman identifies several different sources and dimensions of the synagogue

center: Reform temple, YMHA, settlement house, Jewish school, and Orthodox synagogue.

72. On New York as "Capital of the Jewish World," see Polland and Soyer, *Emerging Metropolis*, chap. 5.

73. Moore, "A Synagogue Center Grows in Brooklyn," 298. The following paragraphs are drawn from this article.

74. Ibid., 304.

75. Kraut, *From Reform Judaism to Ethical Culture*.

76. Waxman and Norden, "Challenge of Implementing Reconstructionism," 194–210.

77. See Gruber, *American Synagogues*, 100–103.

78. Moore, *To the Golden Cities*, 104–11.

79. Mohl, "Some of Us Were There."

80. Naomi W. Cohen, *Jews in Christian America*, 192–97.

81. Moore, *To the Golden Cities*, 178–86.

82. Greene, *Temple Bombing*, 6–7.

83. Ibid., 169–70.

84. Ibid., 237, 267, 329, 380.

85. Moore, *To the Golden Cities*, 269.

86. Quoted in ibid.

87. For a powerful account of abandonment and the struggle to survive, see Kugelmass, *Miracle of Intervale Avenue*.

88. Mayer, "Perpetuation and Growth," 160.

89. Mayer, *From Suburb to Shtetl*; see also Poll, *Hasidic Community of Williamsburg*.

90. Winston, "Cathedral of the Open Air."

91. Heilman and Friedman, *Rebbe*, 158–60. See also Fishkoff, *Rebbe's Army*.

92. Heilman and Friedman, *Rebbe*, 175.

93. Goldschmidt, *Race and Religion*, 109–10.

94. See Prell, *Prayer and Community*, 27–28.

95. Katz, *Visual Culture of Chabad*, 145.

96. Katz, "Many Movements of Chabad."

97. Heilman and Friedman, *Rebbe*, 201.

98. Katz, "Many Movements of Chabad," 14.

CHAPTER 2. STREETS

1. Rosenblatt, "How the Lubavitcher Rebbe Lives On."

2. Heilman and Friedman, *Rebbe*, 170.

3. Fishkoff, *Rebbe's Army*, 11–12.

4. Richard I. Cohen, "Urban Visibility and Biblical Visions," 753.

5. On the Italian festa, see Orsi, *Madonna of 115th Street.*

6. Estimates of the crowd ranged between fifty thousand and one hundred thousand.

7. Dinnerstein, "Funeral of Rabbi Jacob Joseph," 297, 275.

8. Goren, "Rites of Community," 49.

9. Davis, *Parades and Power*, 6.

10. Goren, "Rites of Community," 58–61, quotes on 58, 61.

11. Goren, "Traditional Institutions Transplanted," 71–72.

12. Sholem Aleichem, quoted in Goren, "Traditional Institutions Transplanted," 72.

13. There were four stops: at an Orthodox congregation in Harlem, Ohab Zedek, whose famous cantor, Yosele Rosenblatt, sang the traditional hymn to the dead on the steps of the synagogue; at the United Hebrew Charities building on Second Avenue and Twenty-First Street that housed the offices of the American Jewish Committee and the New York Kehillah; at the Educational Alliance on East Broadway, a Jewish settlement house designed to Americanize immigrants; and at the East Broadway offices of HIAS, an organization established to help new arrivals. Kellman, "Sholem Aleichem's Funeral," 290–91.

14. Ibid., 277–97, quotes on 279, 297.

15. Goren, "Traditional Institutions Transplanted," 70–71.

16. Ibid., 71–72.

17. Ibid., 75. Socialist Jews, rejecting Orthodox Jewish ritual requirements, established their own "Cemetery Departments" in such organizations as the Workmen's Circle, a socialist Jewish fraternal society. For recent trends, see Nathan-Kazis, "Jewish Burial Society Radicals."

18. Orsi, "Introduction: Crossing the City Line," 48.

19. See Bayor, *Neighbors in Conflict.*

20. For a full discussion, see Shapiro, *Crown Heights.*

21. Dash, *Shakespeare and the American Musical*, 81–88.

22. Goldschmidt, *Race and Religion*, 75.

23. Orsi, "Introduction: Crossing the City Line," 48–49.

24. For different interpretations, see Diner, *The Jews of the United States*, 57; Sarna, *American Judaism*, 38; Wenger, *Jewish Americans*, 11; Feingold, *Zion in America*, 50.

25. Barnett, "'Hey You, Anti-Semite!'"

26. Orsi, "Introduction: Crossing the City Line," 44.

27. "Unwritten History: Reminiscences of N. Taylor Phillips," *American Jewish Archives* (1954): 82, quoted in Rock, *Haven of Liberty*, 38.

28. On the eruv, see Fonrobert, "Political Symbolism of the Eruv."

29. The last of the functioning ghettos in Western Europe, in Rome, stood until 1885. It was torn down starting in 1886. Other ghettos, such as that in Ven-

ice, were not dismantled but they had ceased to function as ghettos in 1870 with the unification of Italy. On Rome, see Lerner, "Narrating over the Ghetto." On Jewish space in Islamic cities, see Mann, *Space and Place*, 120–23.

30. Gamm, *Urban Exodus*, 184–221.

31. See the map in Rischin, *Promised City*, 77.

32. Polland and Soyer, *Emerging Metropolis*, 12–13.

33. On Atlanta, see Hertzberg, *Strangers within the Gate City*; on Cleveland, see Gartner, *History of the Jews of Cleveland*; on Detroit, see Rockaway, *Jews of Detroit*; on Chicago, see Cutler, *Jews of Chicago*.

34. Heinze, "Jewish Street Merchants," 203.

35. Bluestone, "Pushcart Evil," 287–88.

36. Heinze, "Jewish Street Merchants," 204–6.

37. Heinze, *Adapting to Abundance*, 67.

38. On lived religion as distinct from popular religion, which suggests a divide between high and low, see Hall, introduction; and Orsi, "Everyday Miracles."

39. Braverman, "Emergence of a Unified Community," 73.

40. Hyman, "Immigrant Women and Consumer Protest," 91–92.

41. Ibid., 100.

42. Ibid., 98, 100.

43. Quoted in Hertzberg, *Strangers within the Gate City*, 91–92.

44. Kazin, *Walker in the City*, 51–52.

45. Ibid., 52.

46. Golden, "Some Days Are More Important," 177.

47. Ibid., 177.

48. Rischin, "Toward the Onomastics."

49. Wenger, "Memory as Identity," 4.

50. Blair, "Visions of the Tenement," 62.

51. Moore and Lobenstine, "Photographing the Lower East Side," 37–38.

52. Bluestone, "Pushcart Evil," 293.

53. Trachtenberg, *Reading American Photographs*, 166.

54. For a discussion of synagogues and their portrayal on the Lower East Side, see Kaufman, "Constructions of Memory."

55. Harburg, "From the Lower East Side," 138–39.

56. Tyler, "Intellectual and the ILGWU," 159.

57. Leipzig, *Growing Up in New York*, n.p.

58. Sorin, *Nurturing Neighborhood*.

59. Moore, *At Home in America*, 71.

60. Philip L. Seman, quoted in *Encyclopedia of Chicago*, http://www.encyclopedia.chicagohistory.org/pages/575.html, accessed December 26, 2013.

61. Sanchez, "What's Good for Boyle Heights," 642.

62. See Drehle, *Triangle*, and Stein, *Triangle Fire*.

63. Goren, "Rites of Community," 62–67.

64. Wenger, "Memory as Identity," 4.

65. Wirth, "Ghetto," 97, 94.

66. Moore, "On the Fringes," 252.

67. The phrase comes from the sociologist Sklare, "Jews, Ethnics and the American City," 72.

68. Moore, "On the Fringes," 252–53, 262.

69. Ibid., 255.

70. Prell, "Community," 70.

71. Ibid.

72. Vivian Gornick, quoted in Moore, *At Home in America*, 62.

73. Prell, "Community," 71.

74. Gornick, in Moore, *At Home in America*, 62.

75. Hentoff, *Boston Boy*, 4.

76. Moore, "On the Fringes," 259.

77. Wenger, *New York Jews*, 107–22, quotes on 113–14.

78. See, for example, Rosen, "Four Fateful Years," 63.

79. For a political version of this, see Berman, "Jewish Urban Politics."

80. Quoted in Kugelmass, "Turfing the Slum," 188.

81. Joselit, "Telling Tales," 54.

82. Kamil, "Tripping Down Memory Lane," 227.

83. Ibid., 228.

84. Quoted in Kugelmass, "Turfing the Slum," 184.

85. Quoted in ibid., 189.

86. Ibid., 199.

87. Ibid., 199–200.

CHAPTER 3. SNAPSHOTS

1. It was subsequently published as Schoener, *Portal to America*.

2. Joselit goes on to argue that museums came to offer American Jews a "neutral Jewish space" where they could experience a kind of belonging based on a shared appreciation of art and history, "rooted in the kind of seeing and witnessing that culminated in a heightened sense of affirmation." Joselit, "Best in Show," 146–48.

3. Zurier, *Picturing the City*, 49.

4. Photographers found the Jewish neighborhood irresistible, especially the throngs of buyers and sellers on the city's streets. Even anonymous photographers left behind a record of the outdoor pushcart markets, which Jews introduced to New York City's streets. See Bluestone, "Pushcart Evil," 290.

5. Blair, "Visions of the Tenement," 58.

6. See Alland, *Jacob A. Riis*.

7. Nora, "Between Memory and History," 19.

8. See Gandal, *Virtues of the Vicious.*

9. Riis, *How the Other Half Lives.*

10. Quoted in Alland, *Jacob A. Riis*, 16.

11. Trachtenberg, *Reading American Photographs*, 170.

12. Zurier, *Picturing the City*, 49.

13. Riis, *How the Other Half Lives*, 83.

14. Gandal, *Virtues of the Vicious*, 87.

15. Linden, "Introduction to the Visual and Material Culture," 272.

16. Blair, "Visions of the Tenement," 65–66.

17. Tucker, "Photo League."

18. *Photo Notes*, April 1939, 3.

19. Quoted in Tucker, "History of the Photo League," 174.

20. Hertzberg, "Essay."

21. Vishniac's photographs were published first in Vishniac, *Polish Jews*, and then in a larger volume, Vishniac, *Vanished World.*

22. See the biography of Cornell Capa in International Center of Photography, *Reflections in a Glass Eye*, 211.

23. For example, Woody Allen's self-portrait in the movie *Annie Hall* when he pictures himself as a Hasid in the eyes of anti-Semitic Granny Hall.

24. See Deborah Kass's "Triple Silver Yentl" (1992) of Streisand as Yentl that graces the cover of Kleeblatt, *Too Jewish?*, as well as Kleeblatt's article, "'Passing' into Multiculturalism."

25. Rischin, *Promised City*, 270.

26. Quoted in Koetzle, *Photo Icons*, 144.

27. Quoted in Gutman, *Lewis W. Hine*, 19.

28. I appreciate Andrew Bush's insight here.

29. Hapgood, *Spirit of the Ghetto*, 77.

30. Trachtenberg, *Reading American Photographs*, 168, 166, 203.

31. Banville, "Secret Geometry."

32. Cartier-Bresson, preface, n.p.

33. Kozloff, *New York*, 41.

34. Quoted in Banville, from Clair and Arbaizar, *Henri Cartier-Bresson.*

35. The term comes from the English translation of *Images à la Sauvette*, his 1952 book of photographs. See Kimmelman, "Cartier-Bresson," A20.

36. Helmreich, *Against All Odds*, and Beth B. Cohen, *Case Closed*, attempt to rectify this bias.

37. I thank MacDonald Moore for these insights.

38. Moore and Lobenstine, "Photographing the Lower East Side," 28.

39. Wenger, "Memory as Identity," 4–5.

40. Hapgood, *Spirit of the Ghetto.*

41. Wirth, *Ghetto.*

42. Wenger, "Memory as Identity," 4.

43. Lepkoff, *Life on the Lower East Side*, frontispiece quote.

44. Howe and Libo, *World of Our Fathers*; Baum, Hyman, and Michel, *Jewish Woman in America*.

45. I am indebted to MacDonald Moore for this paragraph's insights.

46. Rice, "Walter Rosenblum," 5.

47. Quoted in Bezner, *Photography and Politics in America*, 236.

48. *Photo Notes*, January 1948, 7, quoted in Ollman, "Photo League's Forgotten Past," 157.

49. Bluestone, "Pushcart Evil," 307–8.

50. Quoted in Rice, "Walter Rosenblum," 15.

51. Lepkoff, *Life on the Lower East Side*, 9.

52. These paragraphs were drawn from Moore, "Walkers in the City," 287–88.

53. Wasserman, "Choreography of the Streets," 37.

54. Spewack, *Streets*.

55. Maddow, "Broken Horizon" and "Interview of Max Yavno," n.p.

56. Greenfield, preface, 5.

57. On bar mitzvah observances in the prewar period, see Joselit, *Wonders of America*; on postwar excesses, see Bennett, Kroll, and Shell, *Bar Mitzvah Disco*.

58. Greenfield, preface, 8.

59. Klonsky, "Trojans of Brighton Beach," 466.

60. Ibid., 466.

61. Prell, "Community," 73–76.

62. Quoted in Bry, *Alfred Stieglitz*, 9.

63. Quoted in ibid., 11. Kodak introduced the inexpensive Brownie camera, costing just one dollar, in 1900.

64. Quoted in Trachtenberg, *Reading American Photographs*, 167.

65. Ibid., 167.

66. Joel Smith, "How Stieglitz Came to Photograph Cityscapes," 322. Smith notes, "The story of *The Steerage* is by now surely the best-known, and least agreed-upon, story in Stieglitz's repertoire" (330).

67. Ibid., 323.

68. "It is amusingly ironic," writes Stieglitz's biographer Richard Whelan, "that Stieglitz's photograph—which is frequently reproduced to represent hopeful immigrants on their way to America—actually depicts people returning to Europe." Whelan, *Alfred Stieglitz*, 225.

69. Koetzle, *Photo Icons*, 137, 136.

70. Joel Smith, "How Stieglitz Came to Photograph Cityscapes," 322.

71. Koetzle calls *The Steerage* perhaps Stieglitz's most famous photograph.

72. Rischin, *Promised City*, 270.

73. Sarna, "Myth of No Return."

74. Koetzle remarks, "Even today, the photograph is regularly misunderstood as a visual witness to the masses of immigrants that were streaming to the USA around the turn of the twentieth century." See, for example, the cover of Marc Lee Raphael's book, *The Columbia History of Jews and Judaism in America*, and the cover of Philip Levine's poetry collection, *The Mercy*, with a title poem that begins, "The ship that took my mother to Ellis Island / eighty-three years ago was named 'The Mercy'" (73). My appreciation to Andrew Bush for drawing my attention to this.

CONCLUSION

1. Prell, "Community," 71.

BIBLIOGRAPHY

Ackermann, Daniel Kurt. "The 1794 Synagogue of Kahal Kadosh Beth Elohim, Charleston, S.C.: Reconstructed and Reconsidered." *American Jewish History* 93, no. 2 (June 2007): 159–76.

Alland, Alexander. *Jacob A. Riis: Photographer and Citizen*. New York: Aperture, 1974.

Ashton, Dianne. "Expanding Jewish Life in America, 1826–1901." In Raphael, *Columbia History of Jews*, 47–69.

———. *Rebecca Gratz: Women and Judaism in Antebellum America*. Detroit: Wayne State University Press, 1997.

Banville, John. "Secret Geometry." Review of *Henri Cartier-Bresson: The Man, the Image and World*. *New York Review of Books* 50, no. 11 (July 3, 2003). http://www.nybooks.com.proxy.lib.umich.edu/articles/archives/2003/jul/03/secret-geometry/. Accessed December 27, 2013.

Barnett, Barbara. "'Hey You, Anti-Semite!' A Jewish Krewe Does Mardi Gras." February 3, 2013. http://www.religiondispatches.org/archive/culture/6783/_hey_you__anti_semite__a_jewish_krewe_does_mardi_gras/. Accessed December 26, 2013.

Baum, Charlotte, Paula Hyman, and Sonya Michel. *The Jewish Woman in America*. New York: Dial Press, 1976.

Bayor, Ronald. *Neighbors in Conflict: The Irish, Germans, Jews and Italians of New York 1929–1941*. Baltimore: Johns Hopkins University Press, 1978.

Bennett, Roger, Nick Kroll, and Jules Shell, eds. *Bar Mitzvah Disco: The Music May Have Stopped but the Party's Never Over*. New York: Crown, 2005.

Berman, Lila Corwin. "Jewish Urban Politics in the City and Beyond." *Journal of American History* 99 (September 2012): 492–519.

Bezner, Lili Corbus. *Photography and Politics in America: From the New Deal into the Cold War*. Baltimore: Johns Hopkins University Press, 1999.

Blair, Sarah. "Visions of the Tenement: Jews, Photography and Modernity on the Lower East Side." *Images* 4 (2010): 57–81.

Bluestone, Daniel. "The Pushcart Evil." In Ward and Zunz, *Landscape of Modernity*, 287–88.

Bolkosky, Sidney. *Harmony and Dissonance: Voices of Jewish Identity in Detroit, 1914–1967*. Detroit: Wayne State University Press, 1991.

Braude, Ann D. *Sisters and Saints: Women in American Religion*. New York: Oxford University Press, 2007.

Braverman, William A. "The Emergence of a Unified Community, 1880–1917." In Sarna, Smith, and Kosofsky, *Jews of Boston*, 65–86.

Brinkmann, Tobias. *Sundays at Sinai: A Jewish Congregation in Chicago*. Chicago: University of Chicago Press, 2012.

Bry, Doris. *Alfred Stieglitz: Photographer*. Boston: Museum of Fine Arts, 1965.

Bush, Olga. "The Architecture of Jewish Identity: The Neo-Islamic Central Synagogue of New York." *Journal of the Society of Architectural Historians (JSAH)* 61, no. 2 (June 2004): 180–201.

Cartier-Bresson, Henri. Preface to *The World of Henri Cartier-Bresson*. New York: Viking Press, 1968.

Clair, Jean, and Phillipe Arbaizar. *Henri Cartier-Bresson: The Man, the Image and the World*. London: Thames and Hudson, 2003.

Cohen, Beth B. *Case Closed: Holocaust Survivors in Postwar America*. New Brunswick: Rutgers University Press, 2007.

Cohen, Naomi W. *Jews in Christian America: The Pursuit of Religious Equality*. New York: Oxford University Press, 1992.

Cohen, Richard I. "Urban Visibility and Biblical Visions: Jewish Culture in Western and Central Europe in the Modern Age." In *Cultures of the Jews: A New History*, edited by David Biale, 731–96. New York: Schocken Books, 2002.

Cowen, Phillip. *Memories of an American Jew*. New York: International Press, 1932.

Cutler, Irving. *The Jews of Chicago: From Shtetl to Suburb*. Urbana: University of Illinois Press, 1996.

Dash, Irene G. *Shakespeare and the American Musical*. Bloomington: Indiana University Press, 2010.

Davis, Susan. *Parades and Power*. Philadelphia: Temple University Press, 1986.

Diner, Hasia R. *The Jews of the United States, 1654–2000*. Berkeley: University of California Press, 2004.

Diner, Hasia R., Jeffrey Shandler, and Beth S. Wenger, eds. *Remembering the Lower East Side*. Bloomington: Indiana University Press, 2000.

Dinnerstein, Leonard. "The Funeral of Rabbi Jacob Joseph." In *Anti-Semitism in American History*, edited by David A. Gerber, 257–303. Urbana: University of Illinois Press, 1986.

Dotterer, Ronald, Deborah Dash Moore, and Steven M. Cohen, eds. *Jewish Settlement and Community in the Modern Western World*. Selinsgrove, Pa.: Susquehanna University Press, 1991.

Drehle, David Von. *Triangle: The Fire That Changed America*. New York: Atlantic Monthly Press, 2003.

Dubin, Lois C. *The Port Jews of Habsburg Trieste: Absolutist Politics and Enlightenment Culture*. Stanford: Stanford University Press, 1999.

Eagle, Arnold. *At Home Only With God: Believing Jews and Their Children*. New York: Aperture, 1992.

Eisenberg, Ellen, Ava F. Kahn, and William Toll. *Jews of the Pacific Coast: Reinventing Community on America's Edge*. Seattle: University of Washington Press, 2009.

Elzas, Barnett A. *The Reformed Society of Israelites of Charleston, S.C.* New York: Bloch, 1916.

Faber, Eli. "America's Earliest Jewish Settlers, 1654–1820." In Raphael, *Columbia History of Jews*, 21–46.

———. *A Time for Planting: The First Migration 1654–1820*. Baltimore: Johns Hopkins University Press, 1992.

Feingold, Henry L. *Zion in America: The Jewish Experience from Colonial Times to the Present*. New York: Twayne, 1974.

Fishkoff, Sue. *The Rebbe's Army: Inside the World of Chabad-Lubavitch*. New York: Schocken Books, 2010.

Fonrobert, Charlotte. "The Political Symbolism of the Eruv." *Jewish Social Studies* 11, no. 3 (2005): 9–35.

Friedman, Reena Sigman. *These Are Our Children: Jewish Orphanages in the United States, 1880–1925*. Waltham, Mass.: Brandeis University Press, 1994.

Gamm, Gerald. *Urban Exodus: Why the Jews Left Boston and the Catholics Stayed*. Cambridge, Mass.: Harvard University Press, 1999.

Gandal, Keith. *The Virtues of the Vicious: Jacob Riis, Stephen Crane and the Spectacle of the Slum*. New York: Oxford University Press, 1999.

Gartner, Lloyd P. *History of the Jews of Cleveland*. Cleveland: Western Reserve Historical Society, 1987.

Goldberg, J. J. *Jewish Power: Inside the American Jewish Establishment*. Reading, Mass.: Addison-Wesley, 1996.

Golden, Samuel. "Some Days Are More Important: A Memoir of Immigrant New York, 1903–1913." In Dotterer, Moore, and Cohen, *Jewish Settlement and Community*, 167–99.

Goldman, Karla. *Beyond the Synagogue Gallery: Finding a Place for Women in American Judaism*. Cambridge, Mass.: Harvard University Press, 2000.

———. "This Is the Gateway to the Lord: The Legacy of Synagogue Buildings for African American Churches on Cincinnati's Reading Road." In *Black Zion: African American Religious Encounters with Judaism*, edited by Yvonne Chireau and Nathaniel Deutsch, 187–202. New York: Oxford University Press, 1999.

Goldschmidt, Henry. *Race and Religion: Among the Chosen Peoples of Crown Heights*. New Brunswick: Rutgers University Press, 2006.

Goren, Arthur A. *The American Jews*. Cambridge, Mass.: Harvard University Press, 1980.

———. "Jewish New York (1920–1940)." In *New Jewish Time: Jewish Culture in a Secular Age—an Encyclopedic View* [Hebrew], edited by Yirmiyahu Yovel, 3:363–77. Israel: Posen Foundation, 2007.

———. "Public Ceremonies Defining Central Synagogue." In *Congregating and Consecrating at Central Synagogue: The Building of a Religious Fellowship and Public Ceremonies*, edited by Elizabeth Blackmar and Arthur A. Goren, 41–79. New York: Central Synagogue, 2003.

———. "The Rites of Community." In *The Politics and Public Culture of American Jews*, 48–82. Bloomington: Indiana University Press, 1999.

———. "Traditional Institutions Transplanted: The Hevra Kadisha in Europe and America." In *The Jews of North America*, edited by Moses Rischin, 62–78. Detroit: Wayne State University Press, 1987.

Greene, Melissa Faye. *The Temple Bombing*. Reading, Mass.: Addison Wesley, 1996.

Greenfield, Lauren. Preface to *Fast Forward: Growing Up in the Shadow of Hollywood*, 5–9. New York: Knopf, 1997.

Gruber, Samuel D. *American Synagogues: A Century of Architecture and Jewish Community*. New York: Rizzoli, 2003.

Gurock, Jeffrey S. *Orthodox Jews in America*. Bloomington: Indiana University Press, 2009.

Gurock, Jeffrey S., and Jacob J. Schacter. *A Modern Heretic and a Traditional Community: Mordecai M. Kaplan, Orthodoxy and American Judaism*. New York: Columbia University Press, 1997.

Gutman, Judith Mara. *Lewis W. Hine and the American Social Conscience*. New York: Walker and Company, 1967.

Guttman, Alexander. "Ezra Stiles, Newport Jewry, and a Question of Jewish Law." *American Jewish Archives* 34, no. 1 (1982): 98–102.

Hagy, James William. *This Happy Land*. Tuscaloosa: University of Alabama Press, 1992.

Hall, David D. Introduction to *Lived Religion in America: Toward a History of Practice*, edited by David D. Hall, vii–xiii. Princeton: Princeton University Press, 1997.

———, ed. *Lived Religion in America: Toward a History of Practice*. Princeton: Princeton University Press, 1997.

Hapgood, Hutchins. *The Spirit of the Ghetto*. Edited by Moses Rischin. 1902. Reprint, Cambridge, Mass.: Harvard University Press, 1967.

Harburg, Yip. "From the Lower East Side to 'Over the Rainbow.'" In Rosenberg and Goldstein, *Creators and Disturbers*, 137–54.

Heilman, Samuel C., and Menachem M. Friedman. *The Rebbe: The Life and Afterlife of Menachem Mendel Schneerson*. Princeton: Princeton University Press, 2010.

Heinze, Andrew R. *Adapting to Abundance: Jewish Immigrants, Mass Consumption and the Search for an American Identity*. New York: Columbia University Press, 1990.

———. "Jewish Street Merchants and Mass Consumption in New York City, 1880–1914." *American Jewish Archives* 41 (Fall/Winter 1989): 199–214.

Helmreich, William. *Against All Odds: Holocaust Survivors and the Successful Lives They Made in America*. New York: Simon & Schuster, 1992.

Hentoff, Nat. *Boston Boy: Growing Up with Jazz and Other Rebellious Passions*. New York: Knopf, 1986.

Hertzberg, Arthur. "Essay." In *At Home Only with God: Believing Jews and Their Children*, photographs by Arnold Eagle, 1–8. New York: Aperture, 1992.

Hertzberg, Steven. *Strangers within the Gate City: The Jews of Atlanta, 1845–1915*. Philadelphia: Jewish Publication Society, 1978.

Howe, Irving, and Kenneth Libo. *World of Our Fathers: The Journey of the East European Jews to America and the Life They Found and Made*. New York: Harcourt Brace Jovanovich, 1976.

Hyman, Paula E. "From City to Suburb: Temple Mishkan Tefila of Boston." In Wertheimer, *American Synagogue*, 88–105. New York: Cambridge University Press, 1987.

———. "Immigrant Women and Consumer Protest: The New York City Kosher Meat Boycott of 1902." *American Jewish History* 70, no. 1 (September 1980): 91–105.

International Center of Photography. *Reflections in a Glass Eye: Works from the International Center of Photography Collection*. New York: International Center of Photography, 1999.

"Jews as a Percentage of all Residents, 2000." In *Religious Congregations and Membership in the United States, 2000*. Nashville: Glenmary Research Center, 2002.

Jick, Leon A. *The Americanization of the Synagogue, 1820–1870*. Hanover, N.H.: University of New England Press, 1976.

Joselit, Jenna Weissman. "Best in Show: American Jews, Museum Exhibitions, and the Search for Community." In Wertheimer, *Imagining the American Jewish Community*, 141–55.

———. "Telling Tales: Or, How a Slum Became a Shrine." *Jewish Social Studies* 2, no. 2 (Winter 1996): 54–64.

———. *The Wonders of America: Reinventing Jewish Culture, 1880–1950*. New York: Hill & Wang, 1994.

Kamil, Seth. "Tripping Down Memory Lane: Walking Tours on the Jewish Lower East Side." In Diner, Shandler, and Wenger, *Remembering the Lower East Side*, 179–211.

Katz, Maya Balakirsky. "The Many Movements of Chabad." *Sh'ma* 43, no. 695 (2012): 13–14.

———. *The Visual Culture of Chabad*. Cambridge: Cambridge University Press, 2010.

Kaufman, David. "Constructions of Memory: The Synagogues of the Lower East Side." In Diner, Shandler, and Wenger, *Remembering the Lower East Side*, 113–36.

———. *Shul with a Pool: The "Synagogue-Center" in American Jewish History*. Hanover, N.H.: University of New England Press, 1999.

Kazin, Alfred. *Walker in the City*. New York: Harcourt, Brace & World, 1951.

Kellman, Ellen. "Sholem Aleichem's Funeral (New York, 1916): The Making of a National Pageant." *YIVO Annual* 20 (1991): 277–304.

Kimmelman, Michael. "Cartier-Bresson, Artist Who Used Lens, Dies at 95." *New York Times*, August 5, 2004.

Kleeblatt, Norman L. "'Passing' into Multiculturalism." In *Too Jewish? Challenging Traditional Identities*, edited by Norman L. Kleeblatt, 3–38. New York: Jewish Museum and New Brunswick: Rutgers University Press, 1996.

Klonsky, Milton. "The Trojans of Brighton Beach." *Commentary*, May 1947, 462–66.

Koetzle, Hans-Michael. *Photo Icons: The Story Behind the Pictures*. Vol. 1. Cologne: Taschen, 2002.

Kozloff, Max. *New York: Capital of Photography*. New Haven: Yale University Press and N.Y.: Jewish Museum, 2002.

Kraut, Benny. *From Reform Judaism to Ethical Culture: The Religious Evolution of Felix Adler*. Cincinnati: Hebrew Union College Press, 1979.

Kugelmass, Jack. *The Miracle of Intervale Avenue: The Story of a Jewish Congregation in the South Bronx*. New York: Columbia University Press, 1986.

———. "Turfing the Slum: New York City's Tenement Museum and the Politics of Heritage." In Diner, Shandler, and Wenger, *Remembering the Lower East Side*, 179–211.

Leipzig, Arthur. *Growing Up in New York*. Boston: David R. Godine, 1995.

Lepkoff, Rebecca. *Life on the Lower East Side: Photographs by Rebecca Lepkoff 1937–1950*. New York: Princeton Architectural Press, 2006.

Lerner, L. Scott. "The Narrating Architecture of Emancipation." *Jewish Social Studies* 6, no. 3 (2000): 1–30.

———. "Narrating over the Ghetto of Rome." *Jewish Social Studies* 8, nos. 2/3 (2002): 1–38.

Levine, Philip. *The Mercy: Poems*. New York: Knopf, 1999.

Liberles, Robert. "Conflict over Reforms: The Case of Congregation Beth Elohim, Charleston, South Carolina." In Wertheimer, *American Synagogue*, 274–96.

Linden, Diana Louise. "An Introduction to the Visual and Material Culture of New York City Jews, 1840–1920." In Polland and Soyer, *Emerging Metropolis*, 255–88.

Maddow, Ben. "Broken Horizon." In *The Photography of Max Yavno*. Berkeley: University of California Press, 1981.

———. "Interview of Max Yavno." In *The Photography of Max Yavno*. Berkeley: University of California Press, 1981.

Mann, Barbara. *Space and Place in Jewish Studies*. New Brunswick: Rutgers University Press, 2012.

Mayer, Egon. *From Suburb to Shtetl: The Jews of Boro Park*. Philadelphia: Temple University Press, 1979.

———. "The Perpetuation and Growth of Sectarian Pluralism: The Case of the Jewish Communities of Boro Park, Brooklyn." In Dotterer, Moore, and Cohen, *Jewish Settlement and Community*, 154–64.

Mendes-Flohr, Paul, and Jehuda Reinharz, eds. *The Jew in the Modern World: A Documentary History*. New York: Oxford University Press, 1980.

Meyer, Michael A. *Response to Modernity: A History of the Reform Movement in Judaism*. New York: Oxford University Press, 1988.

Mohl, Raymond A. "'Some of Us Were There before Betty': Jewish Women and Political Activism in Postwar Miami." In *A Jewish Feminist Mystique? Jewish Women in Postwar America*, edited by Hasia R. Diner, Shira Kohn, and Rachel Kranson, 22–27. New Brunswick: Rutgers University Press, 2010.

Moïse, Penina. *Poems of Penina Moïse*. Charleston: Nicholas G. Duffy, 1911.

Moore, Deborah Dash. *At Home in America: Second Generation New York Jews 1920–1940*. New York: Columbia University Press, 1981.

———, ed. *City of Promises: A History of the Jews of New York*. 3 vols. New York: New York University Press, 2012.

———. "Freedom's Fruits: The Americanization of an Old-Time Religion." In *A Portion of the People: Three Hundred Years of Southern Jewish Life*, edited by Theodore Rosengarten and Dale Rosengarten, 10–21. Columbia: University of South Carolina Press, 2002.

———. "On the Fringes of the City: Jewish Neighborhoods in Three Boroughs." In Ward and Zunz, *Landscape of Modernity*, 252–72.

———. "Social History of American Judaism." In *Encyclopedia of the American Religious Experience*, edited by Charles H. Lippy and Peter W. Williams, 1:291–310. New York: Scribner, 1988.

———. "A Synagogue Center Grows in Brooklyn." In Wertheimer, *American Synagogue*, 297–326.

———. *To the Golden Cities: Pursuing the American Jewish Dream in Miami and L.A.* New York: Free Press, 1994.

———. "Walkers in the City: Young Jewish Women with Cameras." In *Gender and Jewish History*, edited by Marion A. Kaplan and Deborah Dash Moore, 281–304. Bloomington: Indiana University Press, 2011.

Moore, Deborah Dash, and David Lobenstine. "Photographing the Lower East Side." In Diner, Shandler, and Wenger, *Remembering the Lower East Side*, 27–69.

Morawska, Eva. *Insecure Prosperity: Small-Town Jews in Industrial America, 1890–1940*. Princeton: Princeton University Press, 1996.

Nathan-Kazis, Josh. "Jewish Burial Society Radicals Seek Overthrow of Corporate Funeral Industry." *Forward*, June 21, 2013, 1, 4.

Nora, Pierre. "Between Memory and History: *Les Lieux de Mémoire*." *Representations* 26 (Spring 1989): 7–24.

Ollman, Leah. "The Photo League's Forgotten Past." *History of Photography* 18, no. 2 (Summer 1994): 153–58.

Orsi, Robert A. "Everyday Miracles: The Study of Lived Religion." In Hall, *Lived Religion in America*, 3–21.

———, ed. *Gods of the City: Religion and the American Urban Landscape*. Bloomington: Indiana University Press, 1999.

———. "Introduction: Crossing the City Line." In Orsi, *Gods of the City*, 1–78.

———. *The Madonna of 115th Street: Faith and Community in Italian Harlem, 1880–1950*. New Haven: Yale University Press, 1985.

Poll, Solomon. *The Hasidic Community of Williamsburg: A Study in the Sociology of Religion*. New York: Schocken Books, 1969.

Polland, Annie. *Landmark of the Spirit: The Eldridge Street Synagogue*. New Haven: Yale University Press, 2008.

Polland, Annie, and Daniel Soyer, *Emerging Metropolis: New York Jews in the Age of Immigration*. New York: New York University Press, 2012.

Prell, Riv-Ellen. "Community and the Discourse of Elegy: The Postwar Suburban Debate." In Wertheimer, *Imagining the American Jewish Community*, 67–91.

———. "A New Key: Decorum and the Study of Jews and Judaism." *American Jewish History* 90, no. 1 (March 2002): 13–25.

———. *Prayer and Community: The Havurah in American Judaism*. Detroit: Wayne State University Press, 1989.

Raphael, Marc Lee, ed. *The Columbia History of Jews and Judaism in America*. New York: Columbia University Press, 2009.

———. *The Synagogue in America: A Short History*. New York: New York University Press, 2011.

Rice, Shelley. "Walter Rosenblum: Paying Homage through Photography." In *Walter Rosenblum*. Dresden: Verlag der Kunst, 1990.

Riis, Jacob. *How the Other Half Lives*. New York: Hill & Wang, 1957.

Rischin, Moses. *The Promised City: New York Jews 1870–1914*. Cambridge, Mass.: Harvard University Press, 1962.

———. "Toward the Onomastics of the Great New York Ghetto: How the Lower East Side Got Its Name." In Diner, Shandler, and Wenger, *Remembering the Lower East Side*, 13–27.

Rock, Howard B. *Haven of Liberty: New York Jews in the New World, 1654–1865*. New York: New York University Press, 2012.

Rockaway, Robert A. *The Jews of Detroit: From the Beginning, 1762–1914*. Detroit: Wayne State University Press, 1986.

Rogow, Faith. *Gone to Another Meeting: The National Council of Jewish Women, 1893–1993*. Tuscaloosa: University of Alabama Press, 1993.

Rosen, Philip. "Four Fateful Years: Philadelphia's Jews and the Creation of the State of Israel." In *Philadelphia Jewish Life 1940–1985*, edited by Murray Friedman, 59–80. Ardmore, Pa.: Seth Press, 1986.

Rosenberg, Bernard, and Ernest Goldstein, eds. *Creators and Disturbers: Reminiscences by Jewish Intellectuals of New York*. New York: Columbia University Press, 1982.

Rosenblatt, Gary. "How the Lubavitcher Rebbe Lives On." *Jewish Week*, June 8, 2010.

Sanchez, George. "'What's Good for Boyle Heights Is Good for the Jews': Creating Multiculturalism on the East Side during the 1950s." *American Quarterly* 56, no. 3 (September 2004): 633–61.

Sarna, Jonathan D. *American Judaism: A History*. New Haven: Yale University Press, 2004.

———. "The Myth of No Return: Jewish Return Migration to Eastern Europe, 1881–1914." *American Jewish History* 71, no. 2 (December 1981): 256–68.

Sarna, Jonathan D., Ellen Smith, and Scott-Martin Kosofsky, eds. *Jews of Boston*. New Haven: Yale University Press, and Combined Jewish Philanthropies of Greater Boston, 2005.

Schappes, Morris U., ed. *A Documentary History of the Jews in the United States 1654–1875*. New York: Schocken Books, 1971.

Schoener, Allon. *Portal to America: The Lower East Side, 1870–1925*. New York: Holt, Rinehart and Winston, 1967.

Schor, Esther. *Emma Lazarus*. New York: Nextbook/Schocken, 2006.

Schwartz, Shuly Rubin. *The Rabbi's Wife: The Rebbetzin in American Jewish Life*. New York: New York University Press, 2006.

Shapiro, Edward S. *Crown Heights: Blacks, Jews and the 1991 Riot*. Waltham, Mass.: Brandeis University Press, 2006.

Sklare, Marshall. "Jews, Ethnics and the American City." *Commentary*, April 1972, 70–77.

Smith, Ellen. "Strangers and Sojourners: The Jews of Colonial Boston." In Sarna, Smith, and Kosofsky, *Jews of Boston*, 21–44.

Smith, Joel. "How Stieglitz Came to Photograph Cityscapes." *History of Photography* 20, no. 4 (Winter 1996): 320–31.

Snyder, Saskia Coenen. *Building a Public Judaism: Synagogues and Jewish Identity in Nineteenth Century Europe*. Cambridge, Mass.: Harvard University Press, 2012.

Sorin, Gerald. *The Nurturing Neighborhood: The Brownsville Boys Club and Jewish*

Community in Urban America, 1940–1990. New York: New York University Press, 1990.

Soyer, Daniel. *Jewish Immigrant Associations and American Identity in New York, 1880–1939*. Cambridge, Mass.: Harvard University Press, 1997.

Spewack, Bella. *Streets: A Memoir of the Lower East Side*. New York: Feminist Press, 1995.

Stein, Leon. *The Triangle Fire*. Philadelphia: Lippincott, 1962.

Tarshish, Allan. "The Charleston Organ Case." In *The Jewish Experience in America*, edited by Abraham J. Karp, 281–315. New York: KTAV, 1969.

Toll, William. "From Domestic Judaism to Public Ritual: Women and Religious Identity in the American West." In *Women and American Judaism: Historical Perspectives*, edited by Pamela S. Nadell and Jonathan D. Sarna, 128–47. Hanover, N.H.: University Press of New England, 2001.

Trachtenberg, Alan. *Reading American Photographs: Images as History, Mathew Brady to Walker Evans*. New York: Hill & Wang, 1989.

Tucker, Anne Wilkes. "A History of the Photo League: The Members Speak." *History of Photography* 18, no. 2 (Summer 1994): 174–84.

———. "The Photo League: A Center for Documentary Photography." In *This Was the Photo League: Compassion and the Camera from the Depression to the Cold War*, 9–18. Chicago: Stephen Daiter Gallery, 2001.

Tyler, Gus. "The Intellectual and the ILGWU." In Rosenberg and Goldstein, *Creators and Disturbers*, 155–75.

Vishniac, Roman. *Polish Jews: A Pictorial Record*. New York: Schocken Books, 1947.

———. *A Vanished World*. New York: Farrar, Straus and Giroux, 1983.

Wald, Ken. "The Puzzling Politics of American Jews." In *Jews & Political Life*, edited by Frankel Institute for Advanced Judaic Studies, 6–8. Ann Arbor, Mich.: Frankel Institute for Advanced Judaic Studies, 2012.

Ward, David, and Oliver Zunz, eds. *The Landscape of Modernity: Essays on New York City 1900–1940*. New York: Russell Sage Foundation, 1992.

Wasserman, Suzanne. "Choreography of the Streets: The Life and Work of Rebecca Lepkoff." In Lepkoff, *Life on the Lower East Side*, 32–43. New York: Princeton Architectural Press, 2006.

Waxman, Deborah, and Joyce Galpern Norden. "The Challenge of Implementing Reconstructionism: Art, Ideology, and the Society for the Advancement of Judaism's Sanctuary Mural." *American Jewish History* 95, no. 3 (September 2009): 195–224.

Weissbach, Lee Shai. *Jewish Life in Small-Town America: A History*. New Haven: Yale University Press, 2005.

Wenger, Beth S. *The Jewish Americans: Three Centuries of Voices in America*. New York: Doubleday, 2007.

———. "Memory as Identity: The Invention of the Lower East Side." *American Jewish History* 85, no. 1 (March 1997): 3–27.

———. *New York Jews and the Great Depression: Uncertain Promise.* New Haven: Yale University Press, 1996.

Wertheimer, Jack, ed. *The American Synagogue: A Sanctuary Transformed.* New York: Cambridge University Press, 1987.

———, ed. *Imagining the American Jewish Community.* Waltham, Mass.: Brandeis University Press, 2007.

Whelan, Richard. *Alfred Stieglitz: A Biography.* New York: Little, Brown, 1995.

Winston, Diane. "'The Cathedral of the Open Air': The Salvation Army's Sacralization of Secular Space, New York City, 1880–1910." In Orsi, *Gods of the City*, 367–92.

Wirth, Louis. "The Ghetto." In *Louis Wirth on Cities and Social Life*, edited by Albert Reiss, 84–98. Chicago: University of Chicago Press, 1964.

———. *The Ghetto.* 1928. Reprint, Chicago: University of Chicago Press, 1956.

Zola, Gary Phillip. *Isaac Harby of Charleston 1788–1828.* Tuscaloosa: University of Alabama Press, 1994.

Zurier, Rebecca. *Picturing the City: Urban Vision and the Ashcan School.* Berkeley: University of California Press, 2006.

INDEX

GEORGE H. SHRIVER LECTURE SERIES IN RELIGION IN AMERICAN HISTORY

1 *Religion and the American Nation: Historiography and History,* by JOHN F. WILSON

2 *The Protestant Voice in American Pluralism,* by MARTIN E. MARTY

3 *The Creation-Evolution Debate: Historical Perspectives,* by EDWARD J. LARSON

4 *Religion Enters the Academy: The Origins of the Scholarly Study of Religion in America,* by JAMES TURNER

5 *The Faiths of the Postwar Presidents: From Truman to Obama,* by DAVID L. HOLMES

6 *Urban Origins of American Judaism,* by DEBORAH DASH MOORE